Voyage
of the
Iceberg

THE STORY
OF THE ICEBERG
THAT SANK
THE TITANIC

Voyage *of the* Iceberg

RICHARD BROWN

James Lorimer & Company, Publishers
Toronto 1983

ISBN 0-88862-656-8 cloth

DESIGN: Brant Cowie/Art Plus Ltd.
COVER : "In Polar Seas" by William Bradford. Private Collection, Boston.
MAP: Barbara Dodge

Canadian Cataloguing in Publication Data

Brown, Richard, 1935-
    Voyage of the iceberg

1. Icebergs.   2.   Arctic regions.   I.   Title.

GB2595.B72 1983   551.3'42'02   C83-098850-5

James Lorimer & Company, Publishers
Egerton Ryerson Memorial Building
35 Britain Street
Toronto, Ontario M5A 1R7

Printed and bound in Canada

10 9 8 7 6 5 4 3 2 1

Contents

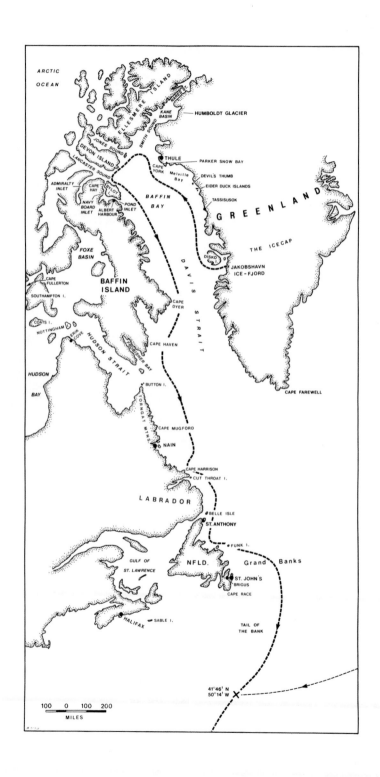

ARCTIC
OCEAN

ELLESMERE ISLAND

KANE
BASIN

HUMBOLDT GLACIER

NARES ST.

SMITH SOUND

JONES SOUND

DEVON ISLAND

LANCASTER SOUND

THULE

CAPE
YORK

PARKER SNOW BAY

Melville
Bay

DEVIL'S THUMB

EIDER DUCK ISLANDS

ADMIRALTY
INLET

CAPE
HAY

ELLOT

BAFFIN
BAY

TASSISUSOK

G R E E N L A N D

NAVY
BOARD
INLET

POND
INLET

ALBERT
HARBOUR

THE ICECAP

FOXE
BASIN

DISKO Q

DAVIS STRAIT

JAKOBSHAVN
ICE - FJORD

CAPE
FULLERTON

BAFFIN
ISLAND

SOUTHAMPTON I.

CAPE
DYER

COATS I.

NOTTINGHAM

ERIK
COVE

HUDSON STRAIT

FROBISHER BAY

CAPE HAVEN

HUDSON

BAY

BUTTON I.

TORNGAT MTNS.

CAPE FAREWELL

CAPE MUGFORD

NAIN

CAPE HARRISON

CUT THROAT I.

L A B R A D O R

BELLE ISLE

ST. ANTHONY

FUNK I.

GULF OF
ST. LAWRENCE

NFLD.

Grand   Banks

ST. JOHN'S
BRIGUS

CAPE RACE

HALIFAX

SABLE I.

TAIL OF
THE BANK

41°46' N
50°14' W   X

100   0   100   200

MILES

Prologue

THERE HAS ONLY BEEN ONE ICEBERG, and its history lasted for a minute. It loomed out of a calm night in the western Atlantic on 14 April 1912, and a minute was all the time it took to rip open the side of the biggest ship in the world, doom some 1,500 people and, incidentally, crack the complacency of the civilized world. *Titanic*'s Iceberg.

The shock of the disaster was so great that we find it hard to think of the Iceberg without a shudder even today—a capricious, icy demon, lying in wait in the dark Atlantic and ready to strike at any passing ship. The truth is less dramatic. The Iceberg was only one small berg among the many hundreds that drift down every spring from Greenland to die in the Gulf Stream. But it had been afloat a great deal longer than *Titanic*, and it was to stay afloat a little longer too. Whatever that fatal minute did to *Titanic*, it was only a small fraction of the Iceberg's own history.

This is the Iceberg's *natural* history, if you like. It is really a set of stories, some of them long, some of them no more than brief images, as the Iceberg drifts through the lives of men and beasts on its long voyage down to the Grand Banks. *Titanic* is only a supporting character in a cast of ships, seals and whales, bears and seabirds, and men as well. What happens to them is often cruel: beast to beast, man to beast, and sea and ice to ships and men. This is inevitable. The Arctic is in many ways a paradise, full of strange men and stranger animals: a bright carpet of flowers in summer, and ice like diamonds in winter. But it is always and forever a hard, cold country, and there is no truthful way to make it seem any sweeter.

This is the Iceberg's story, and *Titanic*'s, from the beginning to the end.

TITANIC
I

IT IS 31 MARCH 1909. They are laying down a new keel at Harland and Wolff's shipyard in Belfast.

Hull 390904 will be no ordinary ship. It has been commissioned by the White Star Line as the second of their new class of enormous passenger liners. The first one is already half-built, a hull on the slips alongside; the third is nothing more than a set of blueprints, so far. All three of them have been designed to carry emigrants one way, and millionaires both ways, across the Atlantic, with all the comforts and amenities appropriate to their stations in life.

This second hull will be a sixth of a mile long, more than ninety-two feet wide at its broadest point, over a hundred feet high from keel to bridge, and another hundred feet on up to the top of its mast. It will have three propellers driven by two huge reciprocating engines and—an innovation—by a turbine of the latest design. The steam to drive all this machinery will come from twenty-nine boilers, fired by the coal in 159 furnaces. The White Star Line expects this massive power to give them a speed of twenty-one knots, and they hope for even more. The ship will have a registered weight of 46,328 tons but, launched and completed, it will actually displace more than 60,000 tons of water.

Quite simply, it will be the largest moving thing ever built by man.

She will be named *Titanic*.

Greenland Ice

And now there came both mist and snow
And it grew wondrous cold;
And ice mast-high came floating by,
As green as emerald.
And through the drifts the snowy clifts
Did send a dismal sheen;
Nor shapes of men or beasts we ken—
The ice was in between.
The ice was here, the ice was there,
The ice was all around.
It crashed and growled, and roared and howled,
Like noises in a swound.

Coleridge, "Rime of the Ancient Mariner"

And as the smart ship grew,
In stature, grace and hue,
In shadowy silent distance grew the Iceberg too.

Hardy, "The Convergence of the Twain"

ONCE UPON A TIME, half-a-million years ago, there was a green country, but it started to snow.

The snow fell very gently in that first fall, as though it hardly meant to. It left nothing more behind than a dusting of white over the land, which vanished into the air as soon as the sun touched it. But the next winter was a little colder and the snow lay a little longer and gradually, imperceptibly, year after year, the winters grew colder still. Soon the snow was falling in storms, and after that in blizzards. After a time each winter's drifts were too deep for the thin summer sun to melt them away, and the next winter's snow made them deeper still. And still the snow kept falling, winter after winter.

Today it is 1910. After four Ice Ages Greenland is no longer green, and not much of a land either. It is nothing more than an enormous mountain of snow two miles high, crushed into ice by its own sheer weight, the land beneath forced down below the level of the sea. All that shows today of the largest island in the world is a ragged fringe of mountains and islands which creep out from under the edges. Greenland is the Ice Cap, a cold and barren waste of rolling white plains, deep crevasses and sharp ridges, with the everlasting winds roaring across it like screaming demons. It is a howling wilderness, and one of the few truly lifeless deserts on earth.

The enormous weight of the Ice Cap bears down on the ice below, and squeezes it slowly into glaciers that come creeping out in tortoise rivers through the fringe of mountains. Today, late in September 1910, the ice that fell as snow a thousand years before Christ was born has come down through the valleys behind Jakobshavn and reaches the sea at last.

But the ice does not stop there. The glacier keeps pressing inexorably forward, sixty-five feet a day, and soon a tongue of ice spreads out into the fiord. It is still only September. The water is warm and so the ice is melting already. Muddy water and a rubble of ice stream away, drifting off down the fiord. Currents surge up the sunken face of the glacier, blasting the fierce miniature world of plankton into the light. Little brown polar cod swarm at the edge of the ice and browse on the tiny shrimps, and flocks of seabirds swoop and dive on cod and shrimps alike. There are big, piratical glaucous gulls the size of geese, almost white in the bright autumn sunshine, and elegant little kittiwakes, grey and white and yodelling. Auks, like miniature flying penguins: big black-and-white murres and small black-and-white dovekies, and black guillemots with feet as red as coral. Fulmars, the

albatrosses of the Arctic, grey and white, or smoky brown. The bleak ice is a desert no longer.

The tongue of ice grows into a long, floating slab, anchored only by the hinge of ice at its landward end. But the hinge becomes more and more precarious as the ice pushes farther out and the tides begin to work on it, up and down, up and down, twice a day. The cracks which run across it soon become crevasses; the crevasses deepen, and the slab of ice heaves and groans under the strain. At last, at one particularly low spring tide, the deepest crevasse breaks through with a roar which echoes off the sides of the fiord like a mountain in labour. The slab crashes off the face of the glacier, scattering the seabirds as it goes. A surge of water, three feet high, runs out ahead of it and batters its way along the walls of the fiord. The Iceberg is launched.

The huge slab of ice turns slowly over, rocks and tilts. It has a tented top like the roof of a house, but an enormous house made for a giant. Its highest point is 100 feet above the water and its lowest is 500 feet below. It is 100 yards long and weighs a million tons. Most of the bergs from Jakobshavn Ice Fiord are like this. The Iceberg is a big one, though not especially big as arctic bergs go.

It is also beautiful; not just white, but sparkling in the sunlight like purest crystal. The sun glances off the infinite facets of a billion bubbles of air, trapped in the snow that fell on the Ice Cap 3,000 years ago. But deep down, in the dark, secret waters of the fiord where the light never comes, the Iceberg is as black as jet, grimed with the dust scraped up by the glacier from a seam of coal, back in the mountains.

The Iceberg is launched. The momentum carries it slowly away, out into the fiord where it gradually rocks itself into stillness. But the Iceberg does not quite stop. Slowly, infinitely slowly, the stream of melt-water takes hold of it, swings it around and takes it down the fiord.

The Iceberg is still in Jakobshavn Ice Fiord at the end of October. The autumn storms from the west have jammed the fiord full of pack-ice from Baffin Bay, and the Iceberg is fixed immovably in it. So are many other bergs, because the Iceberg is only one of the thousand and one bergs that have calved off the Ice Cap behind Jakobshavn in the summer of 1910. It is only one of more than 10,000 very large pieces of ice set adrift in Baffin Bay, circling slowly up to the North Water and the High Arctic, down again to Davis Strait, past Labrador to the Grand Banks of Newfoundland.

The westerly gales roar across the coast of Greenland all through October and it is a long time before they blow themselves out. Then, suddenly, there is one of those bright, uncanny calms of the Greenland autumn, as blue and cloudless as a summer's day; but cold, very cold. And then the still, cold air on top of the Ice Cap begins to sink. It comes rushing down the fiord in a hurricane wind, which blasts the ice-jam back into Baffin Bay again. The bergs begin to move, slowly at first but then faster and faster until they are drifting almost as quickly as a man can walk. The bergs and the pack-ice together come grinding, jostling past the little outport of Jakobshavn and out to sea at last. A last outlier of the Gulf Stream catches them at the mouth of the fiord, deep down, turns them slowly around, against the wind, and carries them steadily off to the north, up the coast to the High Arctic.

There are few human eyes to watch the Iceberg set off on its long, fatal journey to the Grand Banks. But Captain William Adams is

there. He sees it on his way home to Dundee in the whaleship *Morning* with a bumper load of whalebone and oil. Captain Bob Bartlett sees it from *Beothic*, steaming back to Newfoundland from a different kind of summer's hunting, with a safari of wealthy New York hunters on board and a cargo of polar bear cubs, muskox calves and other hunting trophies in his holds. People see it from *Hans Egede* and *Godthaab* as they finish their last rounds of the Greenland trading posts. But all of them see it without seeing, because the Iceberg is only one among hundreds of bergs in the long string spread out along the western horizon, moving majestically northward.

Soon the Iceberg is off the deserted ice coast of Melville Bay, where there are no human eyes to see it at all, nor even any light to see it by. It is December and the sun has set for the rest of the year. There is only the moon and the dim, flickering light from the curtains of the Aurora Borealis.

It is very calm and very cold. The sea begins to freeze.

The sun rises again at the end of January. By then the Iceberg is drifting slowly, aimlessly, in the north of Baffin Bay, starting and stopping with each twist of the current. The sea has frozen very hard, and the Iceberg smashes its way through the pack like a gigantic icebreaker. Sometimes the ice is black and glassy, blasted smooth by the endless wind, with only a few swaths of snow lying on it. Sometimes it is hummocky, with drifts of snow sheltered behind the hummocks. Sometimes it is ridged and buckled from the enormous strains of the wind, the currents and the line of advancing bergs.

It is the deadest time of winter in Greenland. The land is cold, white and empty, with only a few flocks of redpolls in the sheltered valleys, where the dwarf willows poke up through the snow. There are foxes and ptarmigan too, white on white, with smears of bloody feathers to show where the foxes have won. The universal croaking ravens circle above. Nothing more.

It is a different matter under the sea, however hard the blizzards blow above. The ice is full of noises. Cold though it is, the Iceberg is still melting, and the seals underneath hear the faint, fizzling crackle as the imprisoned bubbles break free. The seals themselves call continually: the long, wavering whistles of bearded seals; the clicks, raps and deep, booming bell-like calls of walrus; the barks and yelps of the ringed seals, and the gnawing creaks as they scratch their breathing holes open. Over and under them all, but never quite drowning them out, are the creaks, groans and grinding squeals of the pack-ice in movement.

A sudden and utterly unexpected set of sounds cuts through this strange orchestra: the slither and creak of sledge runners, the yelps of dogs and the voices of men. The seals stop their whistling, clicking and booming as they listen to the runners going past overhead. There are two sledges, piled high with gear, each pulled by a dozen dogs, hitched together in a fan. The drivers ride behind them. They crack their whips, though not very often, because the dogs are happy, running well and need no encouragement. But it is cold, far too cold to ride for more than a few minutes at a time, and the men keep jumping off and running to stay warm. It is so cold that the air freezes the hair in a man's nose, brings tears to his cheeks and freezes them there, and freezes his cheeks as well. The wind whips the spicules of ice into the drivers' faces, and the breaths of men and dogs stream behind them in ghostly plumes.

The two young men riding behind the sledges are hunters from the far northwest of Greenland. They have come over the mountains from the trading post at Thule, across a corner of the Ice Cap, down to the sea ice again, heading for Tassisusok on the far side of Melville Bay. They have more than a hundred miles still to go. One of them is Mitseq, a Sierapaluk Inuit, but the other is a Dane: he is Knud Rasmussen, the pastor's son from Jakobshavn.

Knud Rasmussen is a most unusual hunter, and he is not exactly a typical Dane either. Like most Danes born in Greenland he has his share of Inuit blood, and he is very proud of it; his mother's grandfather was the great Paulus Sealslayer, the most famous hunter of his time. Knud has inherited a boundless fascination with Greenland and its people from his mother's side, while his father has given him a love of classical music and classical scholarship. His Greek is as fluent as his Inuit. Knud can see no contradiction between his two worlds, scholar and dog-driver. His unlikely combination of talents has already earned him a reputation as an arctic traveller and anthropologist, though his friends in Greenland—most of the population—see him rather differently. Knud is a handsome man, witty, articulate, something of a dandy, with a smile which charms every Inuit girl in sight into sewing clothes for him as love gifts.

This winter journey is a small but necessary part of his latest venture. He came north last summer with Peter Freuchen, a footloose young Dane, and they set themselves up as freelance traders. The name of their post is Knud's own idea. "Thule" is Greek for the uttermost northern end of the earth and that, more or less, is where they are. Neither Knud nor Peter is particularly interested in trading as such, but they look on it as an excuse to live in the Arctic. What they really want to do is to use Thule as a jumping-off place for exploring the North and studying the ways of the Inuit peoples. They are going to set off next month on an interestingly dangerous trip across the Ice Cap to northeast Greenland, which is still virtually unexplored. But there is some housekeeping to be done before that. Even part-time traders have to make a living somehow, and Knud and Peter have spent the last six months trading fox furs for rifles, needles and cooking pots. Now they have to get the pile of pelts down to Tassisusok, so that *Hans Egede* can take them back to Denmark in the spring. They have been ferrying these sledgeloads south all winter—the best time of year for travelling in the Arctic—and this is Knud's turn to go. He is in a hurry to get back as quickly as he can, though not just to start off over the Ice Cap. There is a trio of arctic witches back in Thule and he is collecting folktales from them; he wants to finish the job before they all go off on winter journeys of their own. "I have come to look at you and see what you are made of inside," he tells them, and the old ladies cackle with delight. They strike a hard bargain with him: for every story, a ragtime tune on his wheezy new gramophone. "Alexander's Ragtime Band" is their favourite record, and the jaunty tune keeps running through Knud's mind as he, Mitseq and the sledges hurry on past the Iceberg, disappearing into the gloom.

The polar bear watches them go. He is downwind of the dogs, so they do not catch his scent. If they had, Knud would have shot him and added his skin to the load. The bear is an old male, prowling the ice as old male bears do all winter while the young ones hibernate and the females den-up with their suckling cubs. He is hunting for ring seals: delicate little animals, steely grey and blotched like leopards. Most of the ones listening for him under the ice are females ready to pup, but it is still too early to smash open one of their pupping dens to catch his meal. He is hungry *now*, and his only chance is to catch one of the old seals at her breathing hole.

It takes infinite patience. The holes are only an inch or two across and they vanish in a film of ice as soon as the seal has left them. But he has found a hole and lies down beside it to wait.

The seal knows very well that he is up there, somewhere. He weighs over half a ton, so the ice squeaks and groans beneath his slightest movement. The seal has heard him come, against the cacophony of all the other noises around her, and she has not yet heard him go away again. She keeps a network of holes open against just such an emergency, and when she comes up to breathe again she is nearly a hundred yards away.

The bear waits.

The seal is hunting for big shrimps on the underside of the ice, sucking them off one by one. After more than an hour of this her alarm fades away, and her random movements bring her back to the hole where the bear lies in wait. He sees the first tremor of water ahead of her as she comes shooting up. His paw smashes down as she bursts through the thin film of ice. She is still coming up as he bites into her shattered skull and drags her out twisting and thrashing. He growls and worries and rips away at her carcass until his stomach is full. Then he turns away, looking for somewhere to den-up and sleep. He ambles off toward the Iceberg in the complicated way that polar bears have: long and snake-like, his back legs almost over-taking the front. He vanishes into the night.

A raven and a pair of foxes appear out of nowhere beside the raw remains and tug at the thing on the ice which will never now be a pup. Black bird, white fox, bloody snow. The Great Bear—old Arctos himself—wheels slowly and uncaring through the sky high above them, endlessly circling the Pole.

It is the middle of April. Suddenly the bleak winter is over. The sun is up, very low in the sky, but it will not set again until the end of August. The beluga whales which spent the winter as dim, hovering, white shapes moving only to breathe, press forward into every lead as soon as the ice opens up. The foxes bark and the ptarmigan cackle, and both of them moult out of their winter white into their summer camouflage, ready for the latest round in their endless mutual battle to survive. The Arctic is slowly beginning to come alive.

Then the birds come: tight little flocks of yelping oldsquaw, long, low lines of grunting eiders and, very high up, the first skeins of snow geese. Thirty million dovekies pour along the edge of the ice heading for Thule, followed by tens of thousands of murres, kittiwakes and fulmars. Black-and-white snow buntings, just arrived from Europe, sing from every outcrop. All of them are driven on by the desperate need to get in and get breeding, then out again before the short arctic summer is over.

There is also a ship. *Morning* has come north again for the arctic whaling. Captain Adams brings her up along the Greenland coast, picking his way through the thinning pack-ice, until he reaches Melville Bay. There he stops and waits. He is off Devil's Thumb Rock and the Eider Duck Islands where the Dundee whaleships always wait in spring.

Adams has arrived so early because, like every whaleship captain, he knows that the sooner he gets his ship into the High Arctic, the longer he will have for hunting whales. But he has to admit that from a crow's nest view, the prospects look pretty hopeless. The ice beyond Devil's Thumb is an impenetrable jumble of rafted pack, fifteen or twenty feet thick, and certain to crush any ship foolish enough to enter it. Even one as old and as tough as *Morning* which has sailed many times to the Arctic and the Antarctic too. No wonder the old whalers called Melville Bay "The Breaking-Up Yard." But Adams knows what he is doing. Somewhere out there to the north, across a strip of ice that may be a hundred miles wide, or perhaps only twenty, there is an oasis of open sea.

The old whalers called it the North Water. The sea freezes here as fast as it does anywhere else in the Arctic, but the winter gales keep blowing the ice away, pushing it south. There are parts of Baffin Bay that are so clogged with ice that the pack takes two years to melt. Yet the North Water, a stretch of sea as big as Newfoundland or New Mexico and only 900 miles from the North Pole, stays open throughout the long, bitter winter.

When the sun comes back in the spring, the oasis of open water grows even larger. The sea starts to nibble at the ice around it, and the more the ice melts, the more sea there is for the sun to warm. Now, in June, the North Water has spread far west into Lancaster Sound, and is pushing south toward Devil's Thumb, where Captain Adams is patiently waiting and hoping.

With the ice gone now, nothing stops the sun's rays from reaching down into the depths of the sea to make the plants bloom. These are not the ordinary kelps and seaweeds of the shore, but phytoplankton, the real plants of the open ocean: tiny, drifting algae, no more than a cell or two long. Like any earthbound weeds, these need only sun, water and fertilizer to start growing, and there is plenty of each in the North Water in June. Their bloom only lasts a month, but more phytoplankton grows in that short arctic season than in a whole year in the barren tropics. This massive bloom sets off an equally massive swarming of the microscopic animals that graze on it, and of higher predators in their turn. The shrimps are so hungry and abundant by July that their swarms can clean the bait out of a fish trap or the fat off a sealskin, as neatly as any Amazon piranhas. Enormous schools of polar cod, hundreds of narwhal and belugas, tens of thousands of seals, murres and kittiwakes, and millions of dovekies, all gorge on the summer bounty of the North Water.

The bounty also supports a tribe of men—the Sierapaluk and the Saviqsivik. The white men call them "Eskimos," but to themselves, they are "Inuit"—the *true* human beings. They are spread across the empty country from Thule to Cape York. But they do not think the land is barren at all. It is their Earthly Paradise, the only place in the world where *real* human beings can or ought to live. They still half believe what they once knew for centuries—that they are the only people on earth.

By the time the Iceberg drifts past Cape York the pack-ice is looser and studded with bergs of every size and description. The biggest are still the ones from the fiords behind Jakobshavn but there are also many smaller bergs that have crumbled off the ice cliffs in Melville Bay. There are humped and crested bergs, like the backs of dinosaurs; round and ridged ones, like giant scallop shells; tall, turretted squares like castles; tilted blocks which rise to sheer cliffs, like the bows of ocean-liners. There are tent-shaped, conch-shaped, gable-shaped, and fluted bergs. This glittering mass is pushed by the current, stronger now, westward through the thinning pack.

The floes have broken down into pancakes and spicules of ice, and there is nothing left behind but a thin line of slush. The Iceberg brushes it aside and drifts free into the North Water.

TITANIC
II

IT IS 31 MAY 1911, a fine morning of what promises already to be the finest summer of the century.

It is a very proud day for the White Star Line. The company's chairman, the board of directors and their friends have come all the way to Belfast to accept *Olympic*, the first of the gigantic new liners that Harland and Wolff have built for them.

They are launching *Titanic* as well. She sits on the edge of the steep slope beside Belfast Lough, wrapped in scaffolding and bunting, ready to go to sea.

The excitement is enormous. Ten thousand Belfast men have built her up from a bare keel in only two years, and they and their families are all waiting to see the hull of the largest ship in the world slide into the water. The worlds of industry and finance have come to see it too. The grandstand in front of her bows begins to fill up with dignitaries and their wives, stiffly starched and laced—the Lord Mayor of Belfast; Mr. J. Bruce Ismay, chairman of the White Star Line, and Mr. J. Pierpont Morgan, the great American financier who is the power behind the company; and Lord Pirrie, the chairman of Harland and Wolff.

At thirteen minutes after noon Mr. Ismay stands up to make

his speech. Everyone expects him to call on Mrs. Ismay, or Lady Pirrie, or the Lady Mayoress, to swing and smash a bottle of champagne over the bows of *Titanic* to Godbless all who sail in her. But he does no such thing. The White Star Line is a progressive company, and he has no use for these superstitious old seamen's customs. It's the twentieth century, after all. He simply steps up himself and presses a button. It triggers a hydraulic ram which reaches slowly out to push *Titanic*'s bows down the greasy slipway. There are more hydraulic rams to help her on her way but the enormous weight of her hull, empty though it still is, is quite enough to carry her down into Belfast Lough. The platers and riveters and caulkers who are building her cheer and wave their caps as she picks up speed, but their shouts seem oddly muted, overawed by the great red-and-black cliff riding by so high above them. When she reaches the sea a small ripple runs ahead of her, licks the pebbles along the shore and quickly dies away.

It only takes a minute for the restraining hawsers to catch her and bring her to a stop. Then the tugs move in and nudge her onto the dock where *Titanic* will be made into a real ship.

North Water

The Esquimaux from Ice and Snow now free,
In Shallops and in Whale-boats go to Sea;
In Peace they rove along this pleasant shore,
In plenty live; nor do they wish for more.

George Cartwright, "Labrador"

Oh, the look-out up on the mainmast stood,
With a spy-glass in his hand.
'There's a whale, there's a whale, and a whale-fish,' he cried,
And she blows at every span, brave boys,
And she blows at every span.

The captain stood on the quarterdeck,
And the ice was in his eye,
'Overhaul, overhaul, let your jib-sheet fall,
And put your boats to sea, brave boys,
And put your boats to sea!'

Now the harpoon struck and the lines played out,
But she gave such a flourish with her tail,
She capsized our boat and we lost five men,
And we could not catch that whale, brave boys,
And we could not catch that whale.

Oh Greenland is a barren place,
It's a place that bears no green,
Where there's ice and snow, and the whale-fish blow,
And the daylight's seldom seen, brave boys,
And the daylight's seldom seen.

Anon., "The Greenland Whale Fishery"

IT IS JULY: a calm morning in the North Water, the sea a gunmetal grey. The mountains of Greenland, strung along the horizon forty miles away, are blue-black under a roof of cloud.

The Iceberg glides imperceptibly through the thinning mist along a calm streak of water that stretches clear to the horizon. Dovekies come streaming past the Iceberg in flocks of hundreds and thousands, flickering black and white just above the sea. The flocks pitch down along the streak in tight little clusters, like beads on a rosary. They swim about, peering into the water. Then, in ragged synchrony, there is a kick of feet, a flurry of white rumps, and they are gone. The birds drop down into the twilight world ten, twenty fathoms below. They bank and dive through the clouds of plankton, cramming their mouths at every pass. They bob back up into the world of air to sit and flap and catch their breaths. Then they go down again.

There is something else browsing and sieving her way through the plankton, infinitely larger than the flocks of dovekies diving all around her. She is a bowhead whale.

She is a monster—an enormous tadpole, sixty feet long, big, black and fat. Her head is really no more than a vast, sardonic arch of a mouth, with a little eye twinkling at the corner. There is not a single tooth in the whole of that great jaw, but her moustache hangs down inside it instead: the row of frayed, horny strips, ten feet long, that the whalers call her "whalebone." Her nose is on top of her head, and whenever she comes up to breathe she snorts out a high, forked blast of stinking steam that booms like a roll of distant thunder. Her body is wrapped in a blanket of greasy blubber, so thick that her skin scarcely ripples to the straining of the enormous muscles underneath. She tapers down to a tail that branches out into a pair of flukes, twenty feet across. Every whaler in the North Water is afraid of the power of those flukes.

The monster moves slowly along the calm streak, just under the surface, her passing marked by the faint ripples above her ponderous tail. The vast shovel of her jaw drops open and her rows of whalebone swing down. Her mouth is suddenly a cave as big as a whaleboat, and the plankton comes flooding in. She closes it, strains the water out, licks the plankton off her moustache, gulps, and swallows. Then she opens it again.

Sometimes she pauses and calls. It is not the eerie song of a humpback whale, or the squeaks and whistles of a beluga, but a long, low, groaning bellow. It is the call for a mate. This is the time of year

when bowheads languidly roll together, butt, rub noses, gently caress each other with enormous slaps of their flippers; and rise out of the sea in clumsy ecstacy, their bellies joined. It is a call that startles the dovekies that sit and preen just above her, and its echoes travel deep down through the water for scores of miles. She listens, bellows again and listens. But all she hears are the usual noises of ice and bergs, and a low, slow drumming not very far away.

She hears nothing, because there are no bowheads left to answer her.

A century ago, fifty years before the old bowhead was born, the North Water was a paradise of whales. It was a playground where the bowheads breached and blew for as far as a man could see; they leaped so high that the crash of their spray reached a ship's yardarm; they rubbed as tenderly along a keel as though the ship itself were a playmate for courting. But these were whaleships, breaking into the North Water for the first time, and they came to kill, not to play.

The whalers came from English ports like Hull and Whitby, and from Peterhead and Dundee in Scotland, fresh from the massacres of all the other bowheads in the Atlantic, from Spitsbergen to Hudson Strait. They found a bonanza in the North Water, and they slaughtered the whales mercilessly. Men made their fortunes selling the whalebone and the oil from the blubber, both priceless in the age before steel and petroleum. They killed all the big, older "fish" first,

then the young ones, so that by the time the old bowhead was born a man could cruise around Baffin Bay for a whole summer without setting eyes on a single one.

There were only eight bowheads left in the North Water in 1910. Seven of them were hidden deep in Jones Sound, where the whaleships never went. But Captain Adams took *Morning* there, and he killed them all.

Morning is back again in 1911, and the drumming which the old bowhead hears is the beat of the old ship's engine. TUNK-a-TUNK-a-TUNK-a-TUNK. Willy Adams finds it a reassuring sound. He jerks a little whenever it misses a beat, as it often does. It hardly matters on a bright, calm day like today, but this antiquated and rickety contraption may well be the only thing to stand between him and shipwreck. The Adams of Dundee are a famous dynasty of arctic whalers, and Willy has known all about the perils of the North Water ever since he was a child. He knows of the disastrous summers when the pack-ice caught whole fleets of whaleships and never let them go. Of the whalers dying of cold and scurvy on the Baffin ice, with the wreckage drifting home before their wives even knew they were widows. Of the orphans running cold and hungry through the streets. In those days, once a whaleship was nipped in the ice, the only hope of getting her free again was to saw a channel through the ice and try to man-haul the ship to the open water. May God bless James Watt and all the good Scots engineers who put engines into ships and gave us whalers a wee bit better chance of surviving. And may He preserve this old donkey underneath my feet and keep it plodding comfortably on with its TUNK-a-TUNK-a-TUNK-a-TUNK. And may He grant us whales.

The old bowhead is as wary and intelligent as she is old. She has heard that slow drumming before, whatever it is. She has felt it for forty years as a grinding ache in her back every time she dives. She cannot know why, but the tip of a harpoon is chafing against her spine, its steel shaft twisted into a crazy corkscrew by the working of her giant muscles. It is stamped "*ACTIVE* 1871."

It was a bright, calm July day, very like today but not as misty. She lay asleep at the surface, lazily blowing from time to time. She was still very young and inexperienced in those days, and the distant TUNK-a-TUNK of *Active*'s engine was barely enough to wake her. The ship stopped as soon as the men saw her blow, and they had to row quite a distance before they came up to her. There were fulmars on the water all around, pecking the greasy water around her blowhole, even pecking the blowhole itself. The whalers swore, very softly, afraid the bloody birds would wake her up. But the bowhead dozed on, and they slowly rowed into throwing range. The harpooner stood poised in the bow of the lead boat, his line coiled in tubs at his feet. He prayed that his harpoon would hold firm.

His prayers were answered, in a way. He struck the big bowhead square on her back at the base of her tail, and she woke to the pain and surprise of it. She dived at once, rolling headfirst and down. Her big, broad back seemed to roll forever before she stood on her head and went deep. The last thing the harpooner ever saw was the great pillar of her tail rising slowly out of the water beside him, ten, fifteen feet high and far too close, her flukes longer than the whole whaleboat. She lightly flipped a coil of line across his shoulders, but before he could even start to scream her tail came down. In less than five seconds his head was torn from his body and the boat smashed to

kindling. The tail rose up again, snapped the line like thread and tossed them all—men, corpse and broken wood—high in the air. Then she was gone. There was nothing left behind but the whalers struggling in the icy water, a mess of wreckage and a circle of ripples spreading out across the calm summer sea.

Today is different. Willy Adams and his lookouts, and everyone else on *Morning* with an excuse to be above deck, have their eyes peeled for whales. But the sea is covered with patches of mist, and the old bowhead is on the far side of the Iceberg, so they do not see her blow. It would have made no difference if they had. The reason she has lived so long—the reason why she is the only bowhead left in the North Water—is that she is far too wary to be caught again. The noise, and the bright day, and the ache all come together as *fear*. She dives without fuss or panic. Her flukes stand upright for a moment, and then she vanishes.

Morning goes on her way, unseeing, heading up to Jones Sound, and Captain Adams will never have another chance to kill a bowhead. The last whaleship in the North Water never does catch the last whale.

The dovekies above the old bowhead have all finished feeding by the time she blows again and, one by one, the flocks scutter off the water, flying past the Iceberg, toward the mountains of Greenland. They are heading for Parker Snow Bay, set between the smooth, white face of Agpat Sermipaulik glacier and the long, ragged, blue jumble of ice at Pitugfik glacier. The pyramid of Conical Rock, the whalers' landmark, is framed in the pale "V" of the bay, like the foresight of a rifle. Close in, the stark cliffs are not black at all, but crimson from the red lichens covering the rocks, and even the grimy snow still lying in the deep gullies is stained with pink. The incoming flocks cross tens of thousands of other dovekies sitting among the fringe of ice floes at the foot of the cliffs. The sea is now so calm that tiny plankton leave microscopic wakes on the surface of the water, and the image of the cliffs, the Ice Cap and the flying birds in that mirror is marred only by the slow swells and cat's-paws of wind.

The swarm of dovekies comes in high, heading for the plateau between the cliffs and the Ice Cap. They drop down, spiralling and chattering, to the screes on the sides of the mountain. Half of the colony is deep out of sight, brooding their eggs in the maze of crannies underneath the rocks. Their mates cover the screes above, each bird a pepper-and-salt dot beside a pink smear of droppings. The slopes are a chorus of liquid "piuli" calls and high, rhythmic chirrups which merge at a distance into a clacking babble. From time to time there is a sudden silence and a rush of wings like the surge of surf on a beach, as a whole screeful of dovekies erupts in panic before a glaucous gull, or a hunting fox.

The meadows below the screes are brilliant with the new, green growth of tussock grass, starred white and yellow with flowers, which pushes its way through the smoky seed heads and the brown stalks of last summer. Sulphur-yellow butterflies wander from flower to flower. The Arctic is always greenest at places like this, where the droppings of dovekies run off slopes, or over the ruins of long-forgotten Inuit campsites or the gravemound of some long-dead muskox.

The steep cliffs run down to the water's edge on both sides of the narrow bay. Their gullies are bright, sunny wedges of turf where streams trickle down to drop in waterfalls for the last few feet to the sea. The cliffs are a city of many kinds of seabirds. Black guillemots fly in and out of the dark caverns. The nests of kittiwakes climb the slopes from the splash line just above the sea—ragged lumps of seaweed splattered with white, plastered like swallows' nests onto the smallest faults of rock. The murres nest just above them on wide, bare ledges splashed with pink, with rivers of white draining down. At the top—but far below the swarming dovekies that seem no bigger than midges at that height—are the glaucous gulls: a pair to guard each stretch of cliff, their cold, pale eyes alert for any mistake by the lesser seabirds below. The growls of the murres merge into a bee-like murmur, broken by the yodelling "kittiwaa-aaks" echoing up the cliff, and the thin, tentative trills of the snow buntings in the green gullies. A drowsy, pleasant sound on a warm summer afternoon.

The hunting white gyrfalcon comes over the lip of the mountain like an avenging archangel and the whole seabird city scatters in panic before her. She comes down through the twisting dovekies, picks out a murre from the flocks plunging desperately to the sea and safety, turns it and chases it, jinking and twisting up the bay. She hits it with a long, raking slash of her talons, and the body tumbles crazily in a puff of feathers and a spout of blood. The falcon stalls, swoops again and catches it before either blood or feathers can reach the water, flying low and heavily toward the gravel bar at the head of the bay. It is a long time before the birds are back on the cliffs, and the growling and yodelling begin again.

The gyrfalcon crosses the bar so quickly that the eider ducks sitting on it hardly have time to waddle hastily into the water. They stay there because an old man and a boy are coming down the valley, both of them hung about with the bundles of dovekies they caught on the screes to the east. The man carries a net with a long handle, and the boy a handful of snares. They trudge past the end of the glacier at the head of the valley and splash across the wide, shallow stream of melt-water onto the bar. The eiders keep pace with them, grunting in mild alarm. The boy throws stones, aimed to hit them at first and then to skip along the water, but the bar is too high for the stones to skip properly. The eiders stay watchfully just out of range. They are mostly ducks with half-grown broods, whose drakes have long since flown away to the Eider Duck Islands to moult. But one drake is still here, and for a moment he goes into the courting ritual of spring. He jostles behind one of the ducks, rears up, throws his head back, and coos "oo-OO-ah, oo-OO-ah," an ecstatic, unduck-like sound which carries a long way in the calm bay. The boy stops throwing stones and tries to copy the movements, but he is too laden with dovekies to do it properly, so he coos instead. The old man grins and says something about women. The boy laughs and skips another stone.

As they climb up the far side of the valley, a fox barks in protest from higher up the scree. He, too, has been hunting dovekies, to cache for the winter. He stands alert: a little animal, deceptively like a puppy with his round ears and stubby nose; blue-grey, like all the foxes that work the seabird colonies. His wailing bark sounds more like a cat than a fox, and it rings clear against the faraway babble of the dovekies, oddly lonely in the empty valley.

Old Mequsaq and his grandson are Sierapaluk Inuit. The two of them are trudging back to their hunting camp in the cave called Paqitsoq, where the women will do all the things that women usually do to the bundles of dovekies on their backs.

Mequsaq is gnarled and grey, a one-eyed gnome of a man, but he still holds himself like a hunter. His stride up the mountain is as strong as a young man's, and the boy sometimes finds it hard to keep up. His mind is as clear as ever too, and the stories he tells are legendary. He is telling one of them now, to pass the time along the way. It is the story of his life; at least, he comes into it toward the end. He has told it many times before, but it's right the boy should hear it again, so that he can pass it on to his own grandson when Mequsaq is dead and gone. The boy thinks so too.

The story starts so long ago that the old man can only guess at the beginning of it. Once upon a time, perhaps a thousand winters ago, the country beside the North Water was much warmer than it is now. In those first days all the people in the world—all the Inuit, anyway—went wandering east through the Arctic to hunt muskox and caribou in the meadows of Greenland. Then the snows came back. The hard winters killed the caribou, and the Inuit starved. All of them, that is, except the Sierapaluk and the Saviqsivik, who were marooned in this corner of land between the sea and the Ice Cap. Look at it! A man would starve to death here long before he found enough caribou to eat. The stories say the people did starve, many times, but some of them always hung on until the spring, when the dovekies come back as regularly as the sun. The boy knows that less fortunate Inuit manage to eke out a living in places where there are no dovekies at all, because they come into the story later on. But he simply can't imagine what it must be like.

In those years the people of the North Water, lost in their corner of Greenland, passed out of the minds of men, utterly forgotten except in the stories of ghosts, demons and *Tunnit* giants which people like to tell to while away the long winter nights. The Sierapaluk and the Saviqsivik forgot about everyone else in their turn, and for time out of mind they believed they were the only human beings on earth.

Their world changed forever in 1818, when the big white ships came to the North Water. Their Lordships of the Admiralty had requested and required Captain John Ross of the Royal Navy to proceed with HMS *Alexander* and *Isabella*, along with a convoy of whaleships, as far north as the pack-ice in Baffin Bay would permit. He was instructed to determine if there was an Open Sea north of the ice, to report on the prospects for a whale fishery in the region, and to search for a Northwest Passage to the Pacific Ocean. Ross discovered the bowheads and the North Water, though he missed the entrance to the Passage, and he also found the Sierapaluk and the Saviqsivik.

Today, nearly a century afterwards, old Mequsaq can still remember the wonder in the voice of the very old man who was a child when the great white ships came by. They were so huge and their sails so white that they looked like pieces of the moon fallen down to earth, and the strange, white, long-nosed people on board, with their even stranger clothes, must be men from the moon as well. They had long, sharp knives made from metal; sticks that made a noise and killed a walrus from a distance five times greater than a man could throw a harpoon; and shiny yellow tubes to put to your eye and bring a seal so close that you could almost touch it. And *mirrors*! Not one of the Sierapaluk and the Saviqsavik had ever seen his own face before. A world of such magic that old Mequsaq, who has seen many wonders in his long life, still cannot really understand how the white shamans make their mysteries work.

The word of Ross's discovery quickly spread throughout the Arctic. The people of the North Water were not demons or *Tunnit* at all, but real human beings—even though they had forgotten all about kayaks and bows and arrows, and lived mostly on little birds instead of seals and caribou. It made a good story, but not much more. Why should a man travel all that way to a country where there were only birds to eat, when he could live in comfort on Baffin Island and hunt all the caribou he wanted? But it was a different matter fifty years later, when the freezing snow covered the lichens and all the caribou on Baffin died. When a man is starving there's something to be said for eating, even if it's only little birds. And so the white men who were whaling and exploring in Lancaster Sound in the early 1860s began to notice little parties of Inuit passing by, a few dog sledges at a time, always travelling eastward.

This is where Mequsaq's own story begins. He was born on Baffin Island, in what the white men now call Arctic Bay, and he must have been about ten at the time of the great migration. His family followed Kirtaq, the Miracle Man, a shaman of such magic and power that Mequsaq still believes that flames came leaping out of his head to light them on their way. But even the great Kirtaq took three years to guide them to the North Water, the land of the dovekies.

But when they finally reached it, Mequsaq's people did not stay for long. It had nothing to do with eating dovekies, though the little birds were nothing much to boast about and Mequsaq's people said so, often. No, the trouble was that no strange Inuit had visited the

Sierapaluk and the Saviqsavik for generations, and they found it hard to bear the mockery which the newcomers made of their quaint ways. There were times in the next couple of winters when the arguments came to bloodshed, and Mequsaq's people lost. They decided, hungry or not, to go back to Baffin.

It was easier said than done. They set off with very little food, intending to hunt for seals along the way, as travelling Inuit always do, but everything went horribly wrong. Bad snow, bad ice, bad hunting, and they were starving before they were a quarter of the way home. The party fell apart as they got hungrier. The Inuit have strict rules about sharing their hunting kills, but this time the strongest men in the party began to take more than their share, and there was nothing anybody could do to stop them. When all the food had gone, they ate the bodies of the people who were dying beside the sledges. Then they began to butcher the living. They came for Mequsaq's mother while his father was out hunting. The boy fought them off ferociously, but they threw him aside and slaughtered her anyway. They ripped his eye out as well.

There was nothing else the survivors could do but turn back to Greenland and hope for the best. It may be because they were in such desperate straits, or perhaps because there were now so few of them, but this time they had a friendlier reception. The Baffin people repaid it by teaching their hosts how to make bows and kayaks, and how to hunt with them. Gradually, the Sierapaluk and the Saviqsivik accepted them as their own. Mequsaq himself often forgets he was born anywhere else. But he sometimes likes to boast that he has forgotten more about hunting than all the Sierapaluk and the Saviqsavik put together have ever learned. Inuit hunters love to tell tall stories, but Mequsaq's are truer than most.

This is not quite the end of the story, and Mequsaq and the boy still have some way to go before they reach Pakitsoq. But at that moment a ptarmigan, which looks like any other lump of heath, suddenly bursts out from under their feet in an explosion of wings and sails down the valley crowing in protest. She leaves half her tail under Mequsaq's boot, and the boy sticks it in his hair. There are ten eggs in her nest, which the old man and the boy grab for so eagerly that their heads collide. They laugh as they crack open the shells. The eggs are set so hard that there is little yolk left in them, but the tender embryos are delicious. The boy will grow up to be a patient hunter if he eats ptarmigan eggs, says old Mequsaq.

And then? The rest of the story is so recent that Mequsaq can hardly be bothered with it, but the boy insists. The parts to come are about *his* life, after all. So the old man brings his thoughts together and begins again. What happened next was the time when the crazy white men came. Not the *upernatleet*—the whalers, the People Of The Spring. They are crazy enough in their own way, but at least they are hunters; Mequsaq can always understand that. No, these other white men were quite different. They couldn't hunt at all, or drive dogs, or even dress themselves properly in skins. But they still kept going out on dangerous journeys over the ice, to places where there was nothing for a man to hunt and never had been. The people of the North Water found this very hard to understand. When Mequsaq was a younger man he was sure the white men came north just to make love to the snub-nosed Inuit wives, the most beautiful women in the world. Why not? They never brought any women of their own. *Were* there such things as white women? The Inuit talked it over and decided perhaps not; as hospitable hosts, they were glad to lend their own wives instead. But it turned out after a while that they were really after something quite different: "The Big Nail" which the demons have driven into the ice at the northernmost place in the world. That Nail must hold some very powerful magic for them to come such a long way to look for it.

These "crazy" white men were the heroes of the classic age of arctic exploration: Elisha Kent Kane, Isaac Hayes, Charles Hall, George Nares, Adolphus Greely, Frederick Cook, Robert Peary, all searching for a way to the North Pole. Peary was the only one for whom the Inuit had any respect. He was a white man who actually listened to what they had to teach him, and they made him a superb arctic traveller. Peary came back to the North Water so often that they called him "*Piuli*," because he arrived at much the same time as the dovekies, and was equally generous with his gifts. But they were afraid of him all the same, for he was a ruthless man driven by demons. Robert Peary was hell-bent on finding the North Pole and glory at any cost ("The prize of three centuries. My dream and goal for twenty years"), and he was desperate to do it before age, anaemia and crippling frostbite caught him out. He reached it at last on 6 April 1909. But his triumph crumbled when he came home to find out that another American, Dr. Frederick Cook, claimed to have beaten him to the Pole by nearly a year.

Peary's icy fury was awesome, barely sane by anyone's standards, and the Inuit are relieved to know that he and the other white men will not be coming back. Rasmussen and Freuchen are still here at their trading post, of course, but Knud and Peter are so close to being Inuit themselves that they don't count as being white.

Whether Peary or Cook, both of them, or neither, actually reached the North Pole is a topic of highly partisan speculation in the places where these things matter, like New York, London and Copenhagen. Public opinion, which favoured Cook at first, is beginning to run the other way. (As Freuchen puts it, "Cook was a liar and a gentleman; Peary was neither.") But none of this controversy has any meaning at all up here beside the North Water. *What* Big Nail were they looking for? Old Mequsaq knows the men who went there with Cook and the men who went with Peary, and none of them saw any Nail. All the white men did was to travel so far out on the ice that the Inuit were afraid they would never get back to land. When they stopped, they put up a post with a cloth on it, turned around and came home again. And that was *all*? It's very puzzling and nobody, not even Knud or Peter, has ever been able to explain it to Mequsaq's satisfaction. The boy is full of questions too. *Why* would even a white man be crazy enough to go all that way, just to find a Very Big Nail that isn't there?

The old man can only shrug in bewilderment. Life beside the North Water is hard enough as it is, without worrying about foolishness like that as well. But catching dovekies: now, *that's* important. They trudge on up the mountain.

Mequsaq's women sit in the mouth of the cave called Paqitsoq, enjoying the warm July evening. They have been out on the slopes all day—dovekie-hunting is mostly women's work—and there are piles of birds all around, among drifts of feathers. They throw a few birds into the pot for supper, and string the rest into bundles, ready to cache for the winter. One of the girls is stuffing dovekies into a sealskin with its blubber still on; they will make a gourmet meal in the spring when the birds have ripened properly. Her mouth waters at the thought.

The women gossip idly as they work. They talk about old Mequsaq and how he holds his harpoon as upright as ever he did. And what about the white men at Thule, Knud and Peter? What must it be like to make love with a great bear of a man like Peter, the Dane? One of the girls goes into details, and they crow helplessly with laughter. And Knud? (They call him "Kunungak"—"Little Knud.") If he would only let his beard grow like Peter's, it would hide that ugly long nose of his, and then perhaps a woman might pay him some attention? Ah, but there are women no farther away than this cave who might not agree. Look at that one over there? She's sewing a shirt of dovekie skins, soft and tender as a baby's bottom, but it's far too big for any baby. It must be for Little Knud! The girl blushes and looks hard at her sewing. The women all giggle a lot about that.

The oldest woman sits at the edge of the circle and giggles with them, but she has already partly gone away. It has been a long time since she was a fat, flat-nosed beauty, with men fighting over her, and she herself humbly pretending to do what her husbands wanted. The grease trickles down her chin as she chews the fat off the dovekie skins for Knud's shirt. She has been chewing skins into softness for more than sixty years—walrus skins, seal skins, bear skins, murre skins—and by now her teeth are worn down to the gums. It takes an old woman to chew dovekie skins properly, because girls' teeth are far too young and sharp for such delicate stuff. It makes her happy to remember the time when she was a girl herself, and sewing a dovekie shirt like this one as a love-gift. She is very near the end now. One winter, soon, the times will be hard. The food will run out, and she will go off into the snow to die so that the rest of her family can live until the dovekies come back. But winter is far away and there's no point in thinking about it. It's summer now, with plenty of food for everybody, and life is very good. She sits basking in the sunshine, chewing away contentedly.

It is almost midnight, but the dovekies still pour off the screes as they have been doing all day. The sun has gone round to the north, low enough to reach under the clouds and pick out the line of bergs offshore, set against the fogbank. The old woman looks up for a moment from her mumbling. A golden chip of light flashes far out on the southern horizon and catches her eye. Then the Iceberg turns, and the light dies.

TITANIC
III

THE SUMMER OF 1911 PASSES, and *Titanic* gradually becomes a ship.

William James, first Lord Pirrie of Belfast, is far from being a title on the letterhead of Harland and Wolff. Billy Pirrie is a practical shipbuilding engineer who worked his way up from the bottom. He didn't invent mammoth ocean-liners, but he is the man who made them work. He joined Harland and Wolff in 1862 when they were already designing the biggest ships in the world, all of 4,000 tons, and now he's building a beauty like *Titanic*, ten times as big. Where will they go next? Billy Pirrie knows where and how, and his knowledge has taken him all the way up from an apprentice to the chairman of the board.

Shipbuilding engineers are not supposed to have favourites, but *Titanic* is the best ship he has ever built. It's hard to say why exactly, because technically speaking she's little more than a carbon copy of *Olympic*. But Pirrie's small changes have somehow made *Titanic* a sweet ship, elegant and simple. As elegant as a grand master's checkmate, and as beautifully simple as a hole in one. Pirrie is proud of her and if it's possible to love a ship while she's still building, he does.

He watches carefully as the huge shipyard cranes sway her engines down into her empty hull, one by one, followed by her boilers and furnaces, her steering gear and propeller shafts. Then the shipwrights, deep inside her stifling belly, build her decks. They rivet them between the fifteen sections of bulkhead that run across her hull and stretch from her keel to well above her waterline. If *Titanic* should ever be holed, these bulkheads will seal her off into a set of watertight compartments and stop the water from flooding through the whole ship. They ought, in theory, to reach all the way up to her main deck, to give each box a sealed lid as well, but there seems no need for such precautions in a ship as big as this. The bulkheads stop two decks below to leave more room for the first-class accommodations.

Olympic comes home to Belfast in September for a little while and the two sisters, side by side, are a magnificent sight. *Olympic* was sailing out of Southampton when she collided with HMS *Hawke*, a light cruiser. She is back at Harland and Wolff's for repairs to her hull, because theirs is the only dry-dock in the world big enough to take her. Luckily there was no loss of life, and of the two ships it was *Hawke*, the warship, that suffered the most damage. Mr. Ismay and his fellow directors of the White Star Line are not at all alarmed by this accident. In fact, they are privately very pleased. It proves, if proof were needed, the great structural strength and inherent safety of the ships of her class. They are also delighted that *Olympic*'s luxurious comfort is already proving very popular with her passengers. So much so that many of them insist on crossing the Atlantic on *Olympic*, instead of the faster Blue-Riband ships of their archrivals, the Cunard Line.

Titanic's construction is well on schedule, and by the time the summer is over Harland and Wolff have only the upper decks left to build. The White Star Line officially announces that she will sail from Southampton on her maiden voyage on 10 April 1912.

Baffin Island

I have now experience of much of the north-west part of the world, and have brought the passage to that likelihood, as I am assured it must bee in one of foure places, or els not at all.

Report of Captain John Davis, 1587

Now cast your eyes around stern Winter see,
His progress making, on each fading Tree.
The yellow leaf, th'effect of nightly frost.
Proclaims his Visit, to our dreary Coast . . . .
Now Eider-ducks fly south, along the shore;
In milder Climes, to pass the Winter o'er.

George Cartwright, "Labrador"

JULY BECOMES AUGUST, and the Iceberg has drifted across Baffin Bay to the bleak, black coast of Ellesmere Island. The North Water and its riches have been left behind, but by now the Iceberg is carrying its own miniature world with it as it goes. Its underside is furred with algae, red and green. Shrimps and cod swarm in the thickets. Seals and guillemots hunt through its underwater caverns. Fulmars swim above its azure daggers of ice, diligently picking away at amphipods, their heads nodding like chickens. Kittiwakes ride on top of the Iceberg and they swoop down in a shrieking cloud on every over-turned floe, grabbing at the cod left squirming on the ice. The Iceberg is beginning to melt very rapidly. The sound of the bubbles bursting out of the ice is no longer a faint crackle, but a deafening roar.

A strong, cold current from the Pole catches the Iceberg and carries it south along the coast toward Baffin Island. The stream picks up another string of bergs: tall, flat ones from Humboldt Glacier, the biggest glacier in the Arctic, and long low islands of old pack-ice that have been drifting for half a century around the Arctic Ocean. They drift past the dark cliffs of Coburg Island, square across Jones Sound; the sun picks out a bright spike of rock against the black. The kitti-wakes swirling around it are no bigger than motes in the sunbeam. Past Devon Island and its ice cap and glaciers, with Philpott Island buried among them like a Pharoah's pyramid in the desert dunes. Then a loop of current takes the Iceberg out of the pack and into Lancaster Sound, turns it south again, and all but runs it aground on Bylot Island.

Bylot is tucked neatly into the northeast corner of Baffin Island, looking like a changeling brought in from somewhere else: a wall of jagged peaks far higher than the high plateaus of Baffin, which box it in on the west and south. Bylot is dusted with fresh snow even today, at the height of the arctic summer. A round, white dome of an ice cap creeps north through the mountains toward Lancaster Sound and stops there, forever poised to crash down to the sea. But the hidden side of Bylot drops unexpectedly away to the west into rolling brown hills which peter out into a flat, marshy plain. Big, white snowy owls flop along the hillsides and hunt for lemmings, and families of snow geese graze in the steep, green valleys where the streams cut through. Terns, gulls and shorebirds flock on the marsh.

There is a reef across Navy Board Inlet, the western channel between Bylot and Baffin, and the Iceberg comes very close to hitting it before the current twists east, at the last moment. Another berg, grounded on the reef already, stands like a castle, the tide boiling about its feet. Shoals of arctic cod are running into the Inlet, and long lines of hunting harp seals chase them through the tide-rip. Fulmars and kittiwakes circle and swoop, and thousands of murres pour off the cliffs of Bylot. They swerve violently as the Iceberg looms out of the fog in front of them.

The ship coming out of the Inlet swerves too. The Iceberg looms a great deal too close for everyone's comfort, and there are several minutes of frantic cursing before she gets clear again. Then the Iceberg disappears into the fog and drifts back toward Baffin Bay. The ship turns west, steaming deeper into Lancaster Sound.

The ship is *Arctic*, a sailing barque. Close encounters with an iceberg are always unnerving, but she was never in any real danger. *Arctic* is only 436 tons but she is a "wooden wall," solid oak and as tough as they come, built on the same massive plan as battered, old *Morning* and all the other whaleships. But she is not after whales at all. She is a survey vessel, commissioned only ten years ago for the German Antarctic Expedition, though she is now a Dominion government ship on her fourth voyage to the Canadian Arctic.

Once the alarm is over, Captain Bernier goes back to his cabin and settles down to the report he is trying to write. This kind of thing doesn't come very easily to him because he's been a seaman most of his life, ever since he was fourteen. He's been around Cape Horn and the Cape of Good Hope and across the Atlantic many times in the last forty-odd years, far too busy with his navigation and his bills of lading to pick up the knack of writing fluently. To be honest, he'd rather face ice and shipwreck. But reports have to be written, and that's that. What makes it even harder is that this one is a government report and must be written in English. Joseph-Elzéar Bernier is a Québécois from L'Islet in the lower St. Lawrence, and he thinks in French. He looks with mild astonishment at the little pen in his big, scarred fist, at the ugly English words that trail across the paper in the careful script which the Brothers at L'Islet taught him a long time ago.

Bernier is not feeling very pleased with himself this morning, though the Iceberg and the English are only two of the reasons for his discontent. What in the Name of the Good Jesus is he doing up here at his time of life? *Arctic* and he have been north for over a year

now, and he's only just managed to break her out of Arctic Bay, where she was frozen in all winter. It's August, and he still has a summer's work ahead of him before he can go home. Surely it's time he gave up this game for good? God knows his wife keeps begging him to, and God knows he's tried to often enough: as a salvage master, as a dry-dock superintendent, even as governor of the jail at Quebec (his political connections are excellent). But something always draws him to the sea again.

The irony is that his arctic expeditions are entirely his own idea, and if they've gone sour on him now he has only himself to blame. Unlikely though it may seem, this bluff, imperious bull of a sea captain cherishes a private dream. He wants to go to the North Pole. It doesn't matter that Peary and Cook have been there already, because Bernier's dream is part of a far greater ideal. He is a patriot pure and simple, a fervent Canadian nationalist. ("*On est Canayen, ou on ne l'est pas. Deo Gratias.*") No less a man than his Prime Minister, Sir Wilfrid Laurier, has proclaimed that the Twentieth Century belongs to Canada, and what better way could there be to prove it than by raising the Red Ensign at the top of the world?

Bernier has been dreaming of this for more than twenty years, long before he ever saw the Arctic. All the other explorers until then had tried to reach the Pole on foot, or by dog-sledge. But his own plan is

to take a "wooden wall," jam her into the ice somewhere north of Siberia, and let her drift clear across the Pole to the far side of the Arctic Ocean. This, of course, is what the Norwegians tried to do back in 1893-95, with the famous drift of Nansen and Sverdrup in *Fram*. In his more expansive moments Bernier claims he thought of it first. Bernier's dream matched Laurier's ideals so well that Bernier was able to persuade the Canadian government to buy *Arctic* when she came back from the Antarctic (his political connections are *superb*). He was all set to go in 1904, when his orders were changed at the last minute. Word had reached Ottawa that a Yankee whaler, a Captain Comer of New Bedford, was selling liquor to the Inuit in Hudson Bay, and that would never do. The government had second thoughts; surely it would be wiser, Mr. Prime Minister, to send *Arctic* north to look into this problem than on some far-fetched trip to the North Pole?

Bernier has come back to the Arctic on three more expeditions since then, and he is still no nearer his dream. Even though he keeps on hoping, he's slowly coming to realize that nobody is interested in the Pole any more, now that it has been conquered, and that the rest of his career will be spent on nothing more exciting than police duties, mixed with a little surveying and exploration. Dull enough work for a devout nationalist, but it has to be done. Bernier is showing the Canadian flag in the High Arctic, claiming sovereignty over all the lands west of Greenland. The government of Canada has claimed these lands for some time, but it has only just realized that all of the actual discoveries have been made by men of other nations—by the Royal Navy, the American North Pole expeditions and, most recently, by the Norwegian Otto Sverdup in *Fram*. Canada's claim, in other words, is none too sound and Bernier's job is to occupy and make use of these territories in the ways required by International Law.

So Bernier spends much of his time in the Arctic building cairns with plaques that proclaim, to any passing Inuit or polar bear, that these lands are now and forever a part of the Dominion of Canada. He also sells official licences, for a nominal $1 a year, to any whaleship hunting in Canadian arctic waters. He is on his way back at this very moment from an official visit to Albert Harbour to look for customers, but he was out of luck. *Morning* is still up in Jones Sound, where Captain Adams and his men are shooting muskox for lack of any bowheads. *Diana*, an old Newfoundland "wooden wall," has landed her cargo of stores at the Hudson's Bay post, and now she's off on some business of her own—chasing whales in Baffin Bay—Bernier would stake his oath on it. That's the second time he's missed her but, by God, he'll get that damned Newfoundlander before the summer's over, that's for sure.

And that, put a little more diplomatically, brings his report up to date. Bernier knows he has done his duty, and done it well, but it's so far from everything he dreamed of. Now the only bright spot is the pile of letters from his wife and daughter, dropped off at Albert Harbour by *Diana*. Bernier has already been through them once and now he reads them all over again. It must be apple time in L'Islet, and it's over a year since he last tasted an apple, or even saw a tree. It's almost time to go home . . . .

But not quite yet, not for another month at least. Bernier is a proud man who still considers himself an explorer in spite of everything. If he can't sail across the North Pole, he would like to put his name to one last feat of discovery in an Arctic where all the great discoveries have already been made. Nobody has yet sailed a ship around Baffin Island, the third largest island in the world. He knows it can be done. His sledge parties from *Arctic* spent the winter surveying the last unmapped length of the passage, proving beyond a doubt that Baffin *is* an island. It would make a splendid climax to these last two summers in the North, perhaps to his career, if he brought his ship home by this newly discovered route. And that is why *Arctic* heads deeper into Lancaster Sound after she leaves the Iceberg, when instead she really ought to be chasing after *Morning* and *Diana* and selling them whaling licences.

Lancaster Sound is the gateway to the Northwest Passage, and the ghosts of many ships go ahead of *Arctic*. Three hundred and fifty years ago, long before the first Bernier landed in New France, people believed there was a Strait or Passage across the northern parts of the Americas that would take them to the Pacific and the gold and spices of the Indies beyond. The names of the men who tried to find it were a roll-call of the finest English captains in the age of Queen Elizabeth and King James: Frobisher and Davis, Hudson, James and Foxe, Bylot and Baffin. Most of them put their money, and sometimes their lives, on the obvious road: the broad southern entrance to the Passage which begins so promisingly in Hudson Strait but peters out farther west in the ice of Foxe Basin and the enormous *cul-de-sac* of Hudson Bay. Some of the captains found riches: furs, not spices, but more than enough to found the Hudson's Bay Company, and set off a century of small but vicious arctic wars between England and France.

In 1616, Robert Bylot and William Baffin went north instead. Bylot had seen rather too much of Hudson Strait by then. He was Mate on the voyage of *Discoverie* in 1611, when the crew mutinied and turned Henry Hudson and half his crew adrift to freeze in James Bay. Bylot had a hard time bringing *Discoverie* home afterwards, and an even harder time defending himself before the Courts of Inquiry. But he gave a good enough account for his owners—the Companie of Merchants of London, Discoverers of the Northwest Passage—to appoint him Captain. They gave him Baffin, a navigator of genius, and commissioned another voyage in search of the elusive Passage.

The year 1616 must have been a remarkable summer in the High Arctic. Bylot and Baffin brought *Discoverie* up the Greenland coast with hardly a sight of pack-ice, so easily that they had no idea of their luck. They worked their way around the North Water and

probed into the mouths of the great sounds that lead out of it, dutifully naming them for their sponsors: Sir James Lancaster, Sir Thomas Smith, Alderman Sir Frances Jones (his Sound). All of these entrances were wide and free of ice, and any one, they thought, could lead to the Passage. But Bylot, Baffin and the aldermen were doomed to obscurity because nobody really believed their story. None of the ships that tried to follow them could find a way through the jumbled pack-ice in Melville Bay. Nobody cared either, because the Company and the rest of the London merchants were soon making far too much money from the fur trade in Hudson Bay to bother about pressing on to the Indies. And so the charts which had plotted the new discoveries began to register polite incredulity (" . . . according to the relation of W. Baffin in 1616, but not now believed"), and then to leave them out altogether. The remarkable voyage of *Discoverie* was almost forgotten.

After the Napoleonic Wars the Admiralty in London suddenly became very interested in Baffin's old charts. Their Lordships had steered the Royal Navy through a very long war, and they were not at all sure what to do now it was all over. They decided that the best work for a navy in times of peace was to foster the trade of the nation. For the next fifty years this is precisely what it did. Captains who had cut their teeth at Trafalgar and in the American Wars found themselves burning out nests of pirates instead; or charting the horrors of Magellan Strait so ships could avoid the worse horrors of Cape Horn; or taking philosophical gentlemen around the world to measure terrestrial magnetism. This was of particular interest because the compass of every ship in the world pointed to the North Magnetic Pole, and it would be wise to discover as much as possible about this mysterious phenomenon. It promised to be considerably easier to reach than the real Pole. The obvious route to it was through the almost forgotten Northwest Passage, so the Admiralty offered a reward for the first captain to go west of 110° W in the High Arctic.

It was an offer that had unexpected consequences. Without intending to, the Admiralty set off a frenzy of exploration. Britons, Americans, Danes, Swedes, Norwegians, Italians, Austrians and Russians flocked to the Arctic to search for the Passage and then for the North Pole. The search for the Passage cost the lives of Sir John Franklin, the crews of the ships on his 1845 expedition, and of many of the seamen who tried to rescue them. The last link was discovered as early as 1852 but nobody tried to take a ship through the Passage for another fifty years, because it quickly became obvious that the fabulous Strait only led from one icy wilderness to another.

Their Lordships' interest brought the first European seamen back to the North Water since Bylot and Baffin. The captain they chose to lead the expedition in 1818 was a sensible, prudent seaman. Captain John Ross was an old Scotsman, much battered by seas and wars, and a damned sight too sensible and prudent in the eyes of his critics. Ross left his convoy of whaleships to hunt for bowheads in the North Water and pressed on to the west in *Alexander* and *Isabella*. He confirmed everything that Bylot and Baffin had claimed. There was indeed a wide, ice-free channel at the place they had named Lancaster Sound, though Ross doubted very much if it led to a passage. He was sure he could see a line of mountains blocking the Sound in the far distance. But Edward Parry, his second-in-command, saw no mountains at all, and his disgust with the old man bordered on mutiny. Rightly so, as Parry himself proved in 1819, when he sailed 500 miles into the Sound until he was stopped by the ice, not by mountains. But Ross was adamant. He took his ships south instead, and home to England.

Ross had been very lucky with his weather in 1818. Too lucky for his own reputation, in fact, because the summer was so clear that the far arctic mirages looked like solid mountains. He would have been lucky to see Lancaster Sound at all if he had come to the North Water in 1911. This is one of those cold, foggy arctic summers when the ice never clears out of Lancaster Sound. In years like this the seabirds either nest late, or do not try to nest at all. The tens of thousands of murres at Cape Hay, on the tip of Bylot Island, have nested late. Now, as the Iceberg drifts past the colony in the middle of August, their chicks are only just starting to hatch. They are two weeks overdue; perilously late, with the first winter storms only a couple of weeks away.

The Iceberg drifts slowly along the outer coast of Bylot, brushing through the pack-ice. It passes the line of capes and inlets which Ross, like Bylot and Baffin before him, tactfully named for his superiors. Cape Liverpool: the Prime Minister of England (a long, low, undistinguished spit of land which suited the man perfectly). Capes Byam Martin, Graham Moore and Hay: the Comptroller of the Navy, a Lord Commissioner of the Admiralty and, most important of all, their Secretary. Cape Walter Bathurst: a naval hero and an old friend. Pond Inlet: the Astronomer Royal. The Iceberg passes them all on its way southeast.

The short arctic summer is almost over. The butterflies are dying, the flowers are long gone and the tundra is suddenly a brilliant scarlet as the leaves of the dwarf willows begin to turn. There are meadows of berries of every description, and the geese and foxes and ptarmigan gorge on them. The birds are starting to leave, as quickly as they came in the spring. The terns from Bylot Island are halfway to Africa and Antarctica by now. Flocks of snow geese gather in the valleys, almost ready to take off for the salt marshes of Quebec and Chesapeake. Dovekies from Parker Snow Bay flood across to Baffin, and work their way south along the pack-ice. The murre chicks at Cape Hay cannot fly yet, but they launch themselves into the fog and flutter down to the sea, with the hungry glaucous gulls waiting below. Their parents collect the ones which survive; the old birds growl and the chicks pipe back, and together they begin the long swim to their winter quarters off Greenland, 500 miles away. The escape from the arctic winter is well under way almost before the sun has begun to set again.

Captain Bernier is on his way south as well. The ice was too thick for him to force *Arctic* around Baffin, and he has to turn back. It's a bitter moment for a proud man, the death of his arctic hopes. He suddenly feels very old, a failure. Will anybody ever remember Joseph-Elzéar Bernier now, and what he tried to do for Canada in the Arctic? But he has not yet lost his courage and he shrugs off these black doubts as best he can. There's still a job to be done, and he takes *Arctic* back to Albert Harbour. He spends a little time there on police duties, showing the flag, but his heart really isn't in it any longer. He and his crew are homesick for women and families, for trees and green grass. It's definitely time to go home. He takes *Arctic* out of Pond Inlet on 20 August and they are on their way at last.

Bernier's track is the same as the Iceberg's, southeast along the edge of the pack and about fifty miles offshore. He catches up with it just before he reaches Davis Strait—not that he either knows or cares. But what he does see as the fog suddenly lifts is a large berg two miles astern, with a wooden wall beside it taking on ice for fresh water. He has found *Diana* at last, and by the Tabernacle, he's going to make that damned Newfoundlander pay for a whaling licence! He signals *Diana* to heave-to and, to the muted disgust of his whole crew, turns *Arctic* around toward her. But the captain of *Diana* is equally damned if he's going to waste good Newfoundland money on any bloody Canadian licences, and he turns as well. The two ships lumber off through the loose pack-ice at their best speed, but wooden wall engines are grossly underpowered and it is less than a hot pursuit. Soon even Bernier realizes the futility of the chase. He turns *Arctic* back on her proper course while *Diana* and the Iceberg disappear into the fog again.

Diana's crew were taking quite a risk in coming as close to the Iceberg as they did, because it is melting very rapidly and becoming dangerously unstable. The sea keeps nibbling away at it underneath and an endless dribble of ice bobs up in its wake. Whenever the sun breaks through the fog, the melt-water pours down the faces of the Iceberg in glistening cascades. Crevasses open with cracks like gun-shots and slabs of ice crash down into the sea. The Iceberg has lost so much of its mass that its centre of gravity is beginning to shift. It begins to tilt, and its old waterline is cocked some 15° above the new one. Soon it will roll right over.

The moment comes early in September. The Iceberg has reached Davis Strait at last, and the enormous, flat-topped pillars of Cape

Dyer loom out of the fog above it. A sudden gust of wind blasts down through the valleys and catches the Iceberg square on its side. It begins to roll. Very slowly at first, and then faster and faster until it turns over completely and lies gently rocking in the middle of an enormous ring of ripples. A moment ago the Iceberg was a rugged escarpment of ice, not so very different from the slab that calved in Jakobshavn Ice Fiord only a year ago. Now, smoothed and rounded by the water, it is shaped like a gigantic white whale. A streak of frozen coal dust runs across its shoulder like a black ribbon.

The Iceberg, transfigured, drifts on toward Hudson Strait.

TITANIC
IV

HARLAND AND WOLFF have almost finished building *Titanic* by the end of 1911, but there is a great deal still to be done before they hand her over to the White Star Line. Electricians crawl all over her, trailing miles of wire, and an infinite variety of equipment has to be fitted onto her, inside and out: binnacles, searchlights and ventilators, engine-room telegraphs, companion ladders and lifeboats.

Thomas Andrews is in charge of this part of the work. He is the managing director, the man who actually runs the shipyard. Lord Pirrie's nephew, right-hand man and destined heir, Andrews is every bit as good an engineer as his uncle, and in some ways even better, with a genius for detail that never loses sight of the grand engineering design. He also has the happy knack of being as interested in people as he is in shipbuilding. He is as friendly with riveters as he is with peers of the realm, as popular with the Papists as he is with the Protestants in his shipyard. Thomas Andrews is destined to be the master shipbuilder of the new century, as surely as his uncle was of the last.

Andrews' interests as a man and as a shipbuilder are focussed sharply on *Titanic*'s lifeboats. To put it bluntly, there just aren't enough of them. The Board of Trade in London, which governs the safety of British ships at sea, lays down that every ship of over 10,000 tons must carry sixteen lifeboats, and so *Titanic* does. But this regulation is based on an obsolete formula, drawn up twenty years ago, long before anyone ever dreamed of ships as big as 46,328 tons. *Titanic* will have over 2,200 people on board, and sixteen lifeboats can't hold even half of them. It's only a matter of time before the Board brings its formula up to date, and when that happens there will be difficulties. Big though *Titanic* is, she simply is not long enough to carry any more boats if they are to be slung end to end in the usual way, one to each pair of davits. But Pirrie and Andrews are innovative men who can see a way around the problem. They commission an ingenious new design of davit which will carry three lifeboats if necessary, and they fit these onto *Titanic* instead of the standard type.

The problem has been worrying Mr. Ismay and the directors of the White Star Line as well, but they see no reason to install the extra boats until the new regulations make them compulsory. The directors have a responsibilty for their shareholders' investments, after all, and there's no profit to be made out of safety; it's only a formality for a ship as well built as *Titanic*, when all is said and done. But as a compromise, and just to be on the safe side, they add four small lifeboats of the latest collapsible design: hollow, wooden keels with canvas frames that pull up to form the sides. Now there are places for 1,178 people—at a pinch.

As almost the last act of her construction, Harland and Wolff give *Titanic* her funnels. There are four of them: tall, slender and painted in the black-over-buff livery of the White Star Line. They are raked slightly backwards so that, even at her berth, the ship has the air of steaming ahead at full speed.

Titanic is a real ship at last, and a superbly elegant one at that.

Hudson Strait

God created the earth in six days. On the seventh
He sat back, threw rocks at it, and made Labrador.

Newfoundland proverb

November in; the Ships must now be gone,
Or wait the Winter, for the Spring's return.
The Lakes are fast; the Rivers cease to flow;
Now comes the cheerless day of Frost and Snow. . . .
Now blows December with a keener blast;
And Ocean's self, in Icy Chains binds fast.

George Cartwright, "Labrador"

THE HIGH, FLAT-TOPPED COAST OF BAFFIN ISLAND gradually drops away to the south of Cape Dyer. The deep, narrow fiords become wide, shallow bays, with a fringe of reefs and small, rocky islets just offshore to protect them. The reefs are too shallow for most of the big bergs that drift by. A long string of them runs aground off Cape Haven, one by one.

The Iceberg joins the eastern end of the line. The current swirls it around and slams it into the reef. The Iceberg's own momentum drags it bumping and jerking across the shallows. It stops, firmly aground, solid as a rock. Most of the bergs aground off Cape Haven stay there like monuments for years, decades even, until the sea breaks them up and carries them away in a litter of fragments. The chances are that the Iceberg will never float again.

It is the beginning of September and almost winter again. The birds from the High Arctic fly past Cape Haven, hurrying south. The dovekies from Parker Snow Bay reach the edge of the ice in Davis Strait, and the last murres and their chicks are halfway to Greenland. Endless flocks of shearwaters pour away from the coast of Greenland, gorged on capelin; they are sleek, fat and ready to breed on tiny, forgotten islands in the South Atlantic. The long lines pass effortlessly by, swooping and soaring down the troughs of the waves like miniature albatrosses, heading for the middle of the Atlantic and Tristan da Cunha, 6,000 miles away.

The old bowhead comes too. She has worked her way slowly south all summer, nosing in and out of every fiord along the east coast of Baffin. By now, after fifty years of endless journeying, she knows them all. She knows the bays where there is ice all summer and rich feeding along the edge of it, as well as the bays where there is no feeding at all. One of the best places is where the tide-rips roil the plankton over the reefs off Cape Haven but, unaccountably, she hurries past without stopping. There is nothing to alarm her here, not the sight of a ship nor the sound of an engine, but in some strange way the old bowhead smells *fear*. It was here, thirty years ago, that the whalers from *Active* killed her last mate.

Active was not really after the bull at all that day. The big cow was the one they wanted, though they went for her calf first. She would never leave her dead calf, so they were bound to get her as well. But they had reckoned without the bull, who was even more fiercely protective than bowhead bulls usually are. He came charging up to the whaleboats just as the other two turned away, and so he took

their harpoons instead. He dived as soon as he felt the pain, straight down to the bottom, and he hit it so hard that he smashed his jaw. He stayed there for forty long minutes, tongue lolling and jaw bleeding, rolling himself against the rocks as he tried to work the harpoons loose, bellowing in agony. His cries came clear up to the whalers above him, and they followed the cow and her calf for many miles.

The force of the bull's dive took the whaleboat down with him, but the other boats from *Active* came after him, rescued the crew, took up the harpoon line, and belayed it to an ice floe. Then they settled down to wait, watching the floe jerk and bob like a fishing float as the bull writhed and twisted 300 feet below. When he came up at last, wallowing in his own blood, they put another harpoon into him and forced him under before he had a chance to breathe. And another. And another. They played him as a man plays a fish, driving and harrying him, with all their weight on the lines, dragging him to exhaustion. Before the inevitable end came, the bull was carrying seven harpoons in his back, trailing six miles of line behind him and pulling one boat underwater, three more above and an ice floe as well. Even so, it took another full hour before the bleeding and the exhaustion ended him. He came up out of the deep at last and lay there wallowing, too weary to move. The whalers sensed that this was their moment and they began to edge cautiously toward him, harpooners poised to lance him to the heart. But there was no need. He blew a spout of bloody froth and died.

The bowhead bull had been a long time dying, and the whalers were almost as exhausted as he had been. It took a long, weary row to drag his bulky body back to *Active*. It took even longer to cut the whalebone out of him, to peel his blubber off and send it down in bloody lumps to the holds below. Then they turned his naked red carcass adrift to the sharks, the fulmars and the row of foxes pacing hungrily along the edge of the ice. After all their trouble, the whalers were disappointed to find that the bull had been one of those small, frisky fishes—the kind that gives you a lot of grief and nothing much to show for it afterwards. Fifty pounds' worth of gear lost for a load of blubber and bone worth barely a tenth of that. But at least nobody had drowned.

Active is still going strong in 1911. An old, old wooden wall, she was built in 1853, though she was not fitted with an engine until 1871. In her fifty-eight years at the fishery she has hunted whales and seals in Baffin Bay, Spitsbergen, along east Greenland, and even in Antarctica. *Active*, together with Willy Adams' *Morning* and the *A.T. Gifford* of New Bedford, are the last survivors of the great arctic whaling fleets of eighty years ago. *Active* is more of a floating trading post than a whaleship today. The Robert Kinnes Company of Dundee who own her are mainly interested in making a comfortable profit from the seal oil, furs, mica, and walrus ivory which she brings back to Scotland every autumn.

Captain Alexander Murray brought her into Davis Strait as early as he could this spring, as soon as the ice went out. He dropped off his gang of Scots miners to dig for mica in southern Baffin, picked up the local Akolingmiut Inuit and dropped them off with their boats as freelance hunting parties all around Hudson Bay. Now he is taking *Active* on the rounds of all the Kinnes trading posts.

It is an unexpected end to *Active*'s long career, and Alexander Murray can't help feeling a pang of regret. He prides himself on being a hard-headed realist with little room in him for sentiment, and he knows full well that *Active* and all her kind have long since had their day. It was bound to happen sooner or later: in his long life—and he is older than *Active* herself—he has seen the world make more changes than he cares to remember. He began as a whaler, and if he ends as a trader, so be it. But the regret is there all the same. Perhaps it is less

for *Active* than for the days when he was a young man and a hunter, not an elderly captain with rheumatism, poring over his ledgers. Not that he would turn the clock back. Forty years in the whale fishery have been kind to the poor apprentice from Dundee. But there are things he would do differently if he could do them again.

Alexander Murray is a responsible, God-fearing man, an elder of the Kirk and well aware of his duties to his fellow men. He has always tried to be as fair as possible to the Inuit; never cheating them, never plying them with drink or whoring after their women, always liberal with the medicines in his ship's lockers. But the best-laid plans of mice and men . . . . The matter of the Inuit at Cape Low is especially heavy on his conscience. The Saglermiut people who lived there were caught in a strange backwater of time, untouched by white men or even by the other Inuit. They were the last men left, perhaps, of the *Tunnit* people in the old Inuit stories. Murray set up a trading post at Cape Low in 1899 and, unwittingly, brought typhoid along with his other gifts; in only four years every one of the Saglermiut was dead. It is a sin Murray will have to answer for, and it is little consolation that the other whalers' sins are far worse: the Akolingmiut can sing and swear in broad Scots, and they know all about whisky, tuberculosis and syphilis; their children have red hair, or black skins, or blue eyes. They are a monument to Christian civilization which no amount of mission work can ever put right.

Every two or three years Murray spends the winter up north, frozen in at Cape Fullerton on the far side of Hudson Bay, and ready to try for bowheads as soon as the ice breaks up in the spring. But this year Murray will be off home to Dundee as soon as he has picked up his miners and dropped off his hunters. If the Atlantic is kind to him, he will be warming himself by his own cosy fireside before the end of November. After that he'll try one more arctic voyage—just one more bowhead—and then Mr. Kinnes can find another captain for *Active*. And old Sandy Murray will stay by his fireside for ever more.

The Iceberg is still aground off Cape Haven when *Seduisante* and Osbert Clare Forsyth-Grant come out of harbour at the beginning of September. Forsyth-Grant is a Scot, but one of a very different breed from old Captain Murray. He is a laird's son for one thing, the younger son of a wealthy family, and it is odd he should have ended up as a whaler and trader in this frozen corner of the world. On the other hand, he is very much the buccaneering British adventurer who used to go out to far-flung places to found his fortune—and, more or less incidentally, the Empire as well. He is a tough, handsome young man with a sardonic sense of humour, an utter contempt for convention and a set of sceptical opinions which border on Godless anarchy. There are dark whispers among the Inuit that he once murdered another trader for his furs, and though this is not true, it very well might be: he is that kind of man. Visiting missionaries cannot decide if they are more embarrassed by his opinions, the Inuit girl he lives with, or by his ruthless taste for practical jokes. But they have to admit that in spite of everything, they rather like him. He can be a pleasant host when he tries, an interesting man to talk to, and these are prized virtues in the lonely Arctic. Even Captain Bernier likes him, though as a matter of principle, Forsyth-Grant firmly refuses to put his dollar down for a whaling permit.

Forsyth-Grant has been at Cape Haven for a little over a year now, and this is his second hunting season. He prefers the free life in the Arctic to his father's stately home, so he lives here all year round, though he sends his ship home to Scotland in the winter. He is very proud of her. *Seduisante* ("Seddy-santy" to her Dundee crew) is a smart, two-masted barkentine, French-built and with all the elegance that goes with it. Forsyth-Grant has armed her with a harpoon gun in the bows for bowheads, and a smooth-bore swivel gun on either side for seals and walrus. *Seduisante* and the trading post together produced a bumper load last year: 433 walrus hides—hard, spongy leather of the finest kind, up to an inch thick; 23 tons of whale oil and blubber; 659 seal, 414 white fox and 17 polar bear skins; to say nothing of a mixed cargo of walrus tusks, narwhal horns and eiderdown. This adds up to a valuable cargo in 1910, and he hopes to do just as well this year. Before he sends *Seduisante* back to Scotland, he wants to take her into Hudson Strait again to try his luck one more time.

Captain Connon and the other Dundeemen look a little askance at him, because it's getting too late in the year to be taking a ship deeper into the Arctic. It's true that old George Comer still has *Gifford* over on the far side of Hudson Bay, but he is planning to stay there for the winter. Every other captain in the North is winding down his business and going home. *Arctic* is finishing her sovereignty calls; *Active* is picking up her hunting parties; *Stella Maris* is relieving missionary stations; *Discovery* and *Pelican* and *Beothic* have almost completed their rounds of the Hudson's Bay posts. The first autumn gales have begun to blow and it's time for *Seduisante* to get out too. But Forsyth-Grant has heard that enormous herds of walrus come to Nottingham Island every September, at the western end of the strait, and he is hell-bent on trying for them there.

In actual fact he has something much more piratical in mind. He has his eye on one of the chain of new trading posts which have been sprouting like mushrooms along the strait in the last year or two. Last fall, young Ralph Parsons was marooned for the winter at Erik Cove, at the point where the strait turns into Hudson Bay. Parsons was supposed to spend the winter trading for furs and ivory. But Erik Cove is so remote that the Inuit did not discover he was there until spring, so he spent the whole winter completely alone, without even a dog team for company. But intrepid young Newfoundlanders are not easily put off by such trifles, and Ralph patrolled his traplines on snowshoes instead, logging up several hundred miles before spring arrived. It was well worth it: word has gone around all the settlements that he made an exceptionally fine haul of furs in that virgin country. Forsyth-Grant wants it all.

Forsyth-Grant, born of a long line of Scots freebooters, is a free trader who works only for himself, and he has strong views about competition from the Bay. It's muscling in on *his* territory, and he's not going to take this lying down. He's going to sail to Erik Cove just before *Pelican* calls for Parsons' cargo, move in on a dark night (and the nights *are* dark, now it's September), and pick the place clean. Parsons can whistle for his furs for all he cares. The nearest Law is the Royal North-West Mounted Police post at Cape Fullerton, 300 miles away on the far side of Hudson Bay, and by the time Parsons can get word across, his furs and ivory will be to hell and gone and halfway to Scotland. As long as Forsyth-Grant keeps his own head down—he'd be the only white man on board who might be recognized—he can go back to his pleasant life at Cape Haven with nobody the wiser. It simply can't go wrong. He has no intention of harming Parsons, of course, as long as the man behaves reasonably, though he knows that if the worst comes to the worst, his Dundee whalers are capable of absolutely anything. A Dundee whaler will skin his grandmother for her teeth and hide; ask anybody from Peterhead.

Well, not quite anything. Forsyth-Grant is wrong about the temper of his crew, as it happens. Not all of them share his own cavalier views about the ownership of property. That kind of thing was all very well back in the old days but it's 1911 now, for God's sake, and the Northwest Territories are civilized, more or less. Fred Livie, the "baby" of the crew, is only seventeen but he knows his own mind; he's come north to look for money and adventure—but not like *this*. He is not the only one to protest, but Forsyth-Grant is a very persuasive man and he argues all the doubters into agreement, or at least into silence.

And so on 9 September, on a black, stormy night, *Seduisante* slips into Erik Cove. The boats are lowered, and the men row ashore. The place looks deserted, and Forsyth-Grant sees no reason why they shouldn't be safely on their way again by midnight, at the latest.

But this is Forsyth-Grant's second mistake. What he does not know is that Ralph Parsons has had reinforcements. The Bay has bought Parsons a thirty-foot motor launch, *Daryl*, and a couple of keen American yachtsmen on vacation from Yale have just delivered her. Petey Rowland and Bob English collected her from the Grenfell Mission at Mecatina, Labrador, and brought her all the way north—by guess, by God and with the help of a Labrador pilot—much to their surprise and relief. And now they're kicking their heels in Erik Cove for a day or two while they wait for *Pelican* to come and take them home.

It is after sunset. The two Yalemen and George Ford, the pilot, have said their goodnights to Ralph, and they are picking their way down to the beach and the launch. Suddenly there's a tiny spurt of light out at sea where no light could possibly be, and another, and another, all of them moving from east to west. The two Yalemen can't for the life of them think what it could be; a lost hunting party, perhaps—though it's moving much too fast for that. But George Ford is a "liveyere," born and bred "on the Labrador" and wiser in the ways of the coast. *He* thinks that someone is striking matches and flipping them into the water from a moving ship. Somebody lighting his pipe, maybe? Then again, it might be some kind of secret signal to the shore that no one on board can see. But what ship, and why? Something very odd is going on.

Ford and English heave a dory into the water and row out to take a look, they are edging cautiously along the steep cliffs when Ford spots the silhouette of a small sailing ship, and then they both hear the muffled creak of oars. Two boats pull past them, both crammed to the gunwales with men, and it's just light enough to see that they're all carrying guns. This isn't just odd—it's bloody *dangerous*! As soon as the boats have drawn past, English fires off his rifle as a warning; Rowland, back on the launch, starts her up and heads toward them. He has no idea what's going on but, on a hunch, he pushes every switch in sight, and *Daryl* lights up like an excursion steamer.

Forsyth-Grant is astounded, and so are the men in the boats. At one moment they are all alone in the black dark, with the wind and the whistling silence; at the next, the echoes of the gunshot come crashing off the cliff beside them, and the cove is a blaze of light. What the hell is going on? The men in the boats rest on their oars, with *Daryl* between them and *Seduisante*. Forsyth-Grant's mind races through all the possibilities, and he comes up with the obvious answer for someone with a conscience as guilty as his. Of all the *bloody* nights to choose for his raid, he has to pick the one when the Mounties from Cape Fullerton are paying a call. That's buggered it up completely. Whatever the Mounties may or may not prove about his designs on Ralph Parsons and his store, they can quite certainly nail him for illegal hunting. If only he'd bought that damned licence from old Bernier! Now they'll probably confiscate his whole season's cargo, and perhaps *Seduisante* as well, and he can't stand for that. But what the hell can he *do*? He can't fight them off—not even the toughest of his whalers would stand for that—and he can't run away either, not with most of his crew out in the boats. He is trapped and for a moment his nerve fails him.

The Yalemen on *Daryl* are trapped too. It never crosses their minds that they're supposed to be the Mounties; they've no idea there are such people in Hudson Bay. All they know is that they're caught between two bodies of armed men in the middle of what looks very like a pirate raid, and they're outnumbered and outgunned. What do we do *next*, for God's sake? More from desperation than anything else, Petey Rowland tries a bluff. He puts *Daryl* into gear again and roars straight up to the strange ship, hails her in the most authoritative voice he can manage and demands her name. "Seddy-santy," says the lookout—Fred Livie, the secret match-striker—before Forsyth-Grant can shout him down. *And why is she showing no lights?* Forsyth-Grant is taken completely off-balance by this one, and with his mind very much on the Mounties, he can only mumble something about not needing them in this deserted neck of the woods. The authoritative voice has him on the run. But Rowland can't for the life of him think what to say next. After all, the other side has all the guns. There's a distinct pause, and by the time he demands to come on board it doesn't sound very convincing, even to him. Forsyth-Grant has got his courage back again, and he absolutely refuses; to his surprise and infinite relief, the launch turns away. Rowland and English both feel remarkably foolish because their bluff has failed. Forsyth-Grant curses himself, too, because whoever these people may be they're certainly not the Mounties. But he's given so much away that there's now no question of carrying on with the raid. As soon as he sees *Daryl* anchored inshore he signals his men to return. He and everybody else in Erik Cove, afloat and ashore, spend a puzzled and restless night.

Seduisante is still anchored in the cove in the morning, to everyone's surprise. Forsyth-Grant has decided that the best thing to do is to brazen the whole thing out, so he and Captain Connon row ashore to pay a polite social call. He has a great deal of charisma and public-school charm, which he turns on as he sits beside the stove, drinking Ralph Parsons' coffee, and passing the time of day. *Seduisante* has, of course, only put into Erik Cove to take on water, but now he's here he wonders if there's any news of the walrus herds? Parsons has heard nothing. He is equally polite and deadpan in his turn. He says nothing at all about the remarkable events of yesterday evening, but he also makes it quite clear that he's expecting *Pelican* to come in any day now—perhaps even this afternoon? They shake hands, and Forsyth-Grant rows back to his ship, spoiling the effect a little by forgetting to take on water after all. He gets *Seduisante* under way and takes her out into the rising westerly gale.

The same gale shakes the Iceberg free from the shoals off Cape Haven. By now the tides have rocked it, the sun has melted it, and so much ice has broken off underneath that it is poised on a hair-trigger. The gale that comes howling out of Hudson Strait nudges it, tilts it and pushes it back into deep water again. The Iceberg drifts slowly south with the current again, toward Labrador.

Arctic passes it, unknowing, for the third and last time. She is finally going home after two years in the frozen North, and Captain Bernier is not about to stop for God, Canada, Newfoundland whale-ships, or anything else now. He ties up at Quebec at last on 25 September, just as the first flocks of snow geese from Bylot come yelping in high over the city, and whiffle and spiral down to the salt marshes at Cap Tourmente. But Bernier is hurrying down the gangway to greet his wife. He does not hear them go by.

Petey Rowland and Bob English are on their way home too. After *Pelican* took them down the strait, they boarded *Strathcona*, the Grenfell Mission ship, for the trip south along the Labrador coast. Rowland finds his father on board, very anxious about his son's safety. In his relief Dr. Rowland gives young Petey a mild but firm parental earful about all the worry he has caused through this fool-hardy expedition. Petey takes it all very well, ruefully amused to be treated as a schoolboy again after his adventurous summer as the captain of *Daryl*.

Wilfred Grenfell is on *Strathcona* as well. She is his hospital ship, and every summer he goes up and down the Labrador to give the liveyeres in the remote outports the only medical help they will have all year. Sir Wilfred (he has just been knighted) is a medical mission-ary, a hero with a worldwide reputation as the founder of the Grenfell Mission. He came to Labrador twenty years ago for a summer visit, an English gentleman of Evangelical faith. The abject poverty of this forgotten country appalled him, so he stayed on to found the mission. It is his life's work. He now has a string of hospitals, a school and an orphanage to serve his people, and he is their trader and magistrate as well. Grenfell's eloquence has helped him raise the money for his Labrador crusade through his very popular public lectures in England

and America. He charmed *Strathcona*, brand new, from the canny heart of old Lord Strathcona himself, the richest man in Canada. Grenfell's golden words also persuade lesser men to help his cause, and that is how Bob English and Petey Rowland came to volunteer their time for their recent jaunt north, with *Daryl*.

As it happens, Bob and Petey are not the only unexpected guests on board *Strathcona*. There is a rumour of smallpox in one of the isolated outports just down the coast, and Grenfell sails there at once. He finds a man and a woman stretched out dead in their small, ramshackle cabin, with two small children barely alive beside them. Quite indifferent to the danger of becoming infected themselves, Grenfell and Dr. Rowland carry the children back to *Strathcona*. Petey has always admired his father, and he wishes he had that kind of courage himself.

Or any kind of courage, for that matter. There is always a great deal of fog on the Labrador in summer but it begins to lift in September, and the two Yaleman are only now seeing the country for the first time. Neither of them say anything to Petey's father, but secretly they are both horrified. The rugged coast looks dangerous enough from *Strathcona*, and they can only thank God they never saw it properly from *Daryl*. It's nothing much to begin with: the little Button Islands at the northern tip are no more than a maze of low, rocky cliffs, with the tide boiling through them. But gradually, mile by mile, the rocks loom higher and higher until they build into the Torngat mountains: saw-toothed, bleak and utterly barren, looking much as they did when the last Ice Age left them behind. By the time the range ends at Cape Mugford, 150 miles south of Hudson Strait, the mountains of Labrador are the highest peaks east of the Rockies, climbing 4,000 feet straight up out of the sea and towering impossibly high above *Strathcona*. They are unexplored, and the whole coast is virtually uncharted too—and the little that's on the charts is mostly wrong. The skippers who sail their schooners down from Newfoundland for the summer fishing feel their way along it from headland to headland; they have an interminable bit of doggerel which sets out all the leading marks to look out for. George Ford tried to teach it to Petey on the way north in *Daryl* but, as Petey quickly discovered, rhymes don't help much when the fog is thick enough to cut in slices and spread on bread. The fierce tide-rips in the narrow channels, and the whirlwinds that tear down through the gaps in the Torngats don't help very much either. Rowland and English now see

that they were very lucky to bring a launch as small as *Daryl* all the way up that coast, and very foolish even to try. One of the more dangerous channels they passed is called Run-by-Guess. It sums up their experience perfectly.

Fifteen hundred miles farther west, another shipload of young men is running-by-guess too. They have been surveying in Hudson Bay, and they are desperately trying to escape, ahead of the ice and the storms. Their ship is a schooner, *Chrissie M. Thomey*, out of Brigus, Newfoundland, and the crew have spent the summer charting the approaches to Churchill, Manitoba, at the bottom of the bay. (There is talk of building a railroad there to ship grain out of the Prairies.) *Thomey* finally got away on 23 September and she is limping home as fast as they can make her go, with a bad leak and a doubtful engine. The crew are very tired, and they are just beginning to be afraid. Their ship is so frail that they feel horribly vulnerable.

Thomey reaches the western end of Hudson Strait on 29 September, in the middle of a snowstorm so thick that she is running blind.

The lookout on her bow is Bob Fraser, a young surveyor, and he is astounded to see another sailing ship loom out of the snow beside him, almost at arm's length—and instantly vanish again, like some arctic Flying Dutchman. He rubs his tired eyes, thinking it's a trick of the swirling snow. But he is wrong. There was a ship, and she is *Seduisante*.

Osbert Clare Forsyth-Grant is not the kind of man to be abashed after his fiasco at Erik Cove. He is set on sending a bumper cargo back to Scotland, and if he can't get it by piracy, then he'll just have to hunt for it. The trouble is that he doesn't know where to go. He has spent the last three weeks criss-crossing the western end of Hudson Strait, without seeing the least sign of any walrus. He put in at Digges Island, just west of Erik Cove, where he found *Active*. In the careful, roundabout way of all rival hunters and fishermen Forsyth-Grant and Captain Murray pumped each other cautiously for information. Predictably enough, neither gave anything away.

The promised herds of walrus have not yet come to Nottingham Island, or anywhere else as far as Forsyth-Grant can see. His crew are getting restless as the weather worsens. It's all very well for the boss to stay out here so late in the year. *He* is only going home to his girl at Cape Haven, while *we* have to cross the bloody ocean to Dundee, and that's no joke in October in a wee ship like *Seduisante*. But Forsyth-Grant is as persuasive as ever, and they reluctantly agree to sail back to take one last look at Nottingham. They are on their way there when *Chrissie M. Thomey* passes them in the snow.

Forsyth-Grant is as startled as Bob Fraser by their narrow miss, but he soon shrugs it off; a miss is as good as a mile. What matters now is that the wind has dropped during the night and the snow is lifting. It looks good. He brings *Seduisante* around the northern point of Nottingham early in the afternoon, and whoops with delight. He sees a big square head and a vast, soft, leathery brown back bob up in front of him, and the walrus snorts out a spatter of clam shells. There are dozens of the animals in the shallows ahead of him, all snorting and spattering; this nearest one is almost within gunshot. But the walrus sees the ship just as the swivel-gunner draws a bead on him, and he dives at once. The shot is too late. It only serves to warn the rest of the herd and they dive as well, in widening circles of panic. When they come up again they are some way ahead of *Seduisante* in a tight pack, rolling and porpoising as they go, in the clumsy walrus parody of how seals swim.

Forsyth-Grant takes after them with a yell, the wind behind him and the engine at full throttle. The hell with shoal water. There's a man at the harpoon gun, and one at each of the swivels. The rest of the crew, Dundee whalers and Inuit hunters alike, crane forward over the bulwarks with their rifles aimed, all of them cheering crazily. The walrus are almost within gunshot but they suddenly turn into the channel between the main island and one of the outlying rocks. *Seduisante* turns after them.

She jerks. Then she shudders. She jerks again, and the sound of her engine winds up into a banshee scream. Then she comes to a long, scraping, jolting stop, her crew tumbling forward and grabbing at anything in reach, with half the foremast falling on top of them. *Seduisante* is firmly aground, as the engine dies in a blast of steam. The crew pick themselves up and look at each other. The Dundee men begin to swear—but only very softly, in the way people do when it really matters. It is clear to all of them that they are nearly as good as dead. *Seduisante* is hard aground, with half her foremast gone and something very wrong with her engine, and Christ alone knows how much damage down below. It is the beginning of winter, and there is no chance at all of another ship coming to their rescue. And the wind is getting up again.

There are only two ways out of this mess, and neither of them holds much hope. The first is to stay with the ship and hope she will float off again tonight, at high tide. After all, she's built for arctic work, and she can't have taken much harm from a little bump like that. That's what Forsyth-Grant says. But the Dundee whalers want nothing more to do with the bloody man. They want to go home *now*, even if they have to put Jesus Boots on and *walk* there. They say so repeatedly, and their anger rises every time. But the trouble with walking, Forsyth-Grant keeps shouting back, is that *there's no ice yet*, and *there won't bloody be any* for another month at least. And it's *too bloody dangerous* to send a whaleboat across the strait to get help. *Stay with the ship*—or do you really want to sit on your arses on Nottingham and *starve*? He tries to shout them all down, with his usual mixture of Scots obscenities and aristocratic arrogance, but this time it doesn't work. After a while he agrees, grudgingly, to send all the Inuit off in their skin boats in search of help. God knows that if anything does go wrong it would be better to have them on shore. But he absolutely refuses to let anybody else go with them. Little Fred Livie makes a jump for one of the boats as it pulls away but Forsyth-Grant hauls him out, thumps him and leaves him whimpering in the scuppers. Then the arguments begin again.

The last the Inuit hear of Forsyth-Grant is his bellow outshouting all the others. It is dark by the time they get to the island, and they see nothing more of him, the ship or anything else. But they can hear gusts of shouting from time to time as they huddle among the rocks over a driftwood fire, and sometimes drunken singing, and once a couple of shots. (Perhaps the boss has shot a couple of mutineers? Or maybe they have shot him? The Inuit argue about it now and end-lessly, all through the long winter marooned on Nottingham.) They can also hear *Seduisante* beginning to stir as the tide rises and the sea slams into the cove; *BOOM* and grind against the rocks, and *BOOM* again. After a while all these noises are blotted out by the surf and the rising gale.

By daybreak *Seduisante* is nothing more than a jumble of drifting ropes and timbers. Osbert Clare Forsyth-Grant and all his crew are dead.

The Iceberg is far down the Labrador coast by now, drifting along the outer edge of the banks. It is a little north of Run-by-Guess when the twist of an eddy brings it in again. The sea has been steadily nibbling at it, but the Iceberg is still too deep to float in 150 feet of water. It gouges a great trough through the silt on Harrison Bank and grinds to a stop for the second time.

Cape Harrison and the hills behind it loom on the horizon thirty miles to the west, but they are not the stark, jagged moonscape of the Torngat country. This part of Labrador is flatter and more rolling, covered with lakes, spruce trees and barrens where the caribou graze. A gentler land, but not by one single inch a more forgiving one. It is still the same harsh, cold country, invincibly protected by the bitter winter, and its own impenetrable shield of mosquitos, deerflies and blackflies all summer. It is still the same unexplored wilderness. It seems strange in this modern world of 1911, when the Frontier has been closed and all the virgin land of America tamed, that there should be a place no farther north than Scotland that is as mysterious as Antarctica or the steppes of Central Asia.

But this is not quite true of the coast. Fishermen and the occasional pirate have worked along it for centuries, and though the charts may be wrong, at least there *are* charts. This entire stretch of shore is dotted with harbours and little settlements—trading posts, liveyere shacks, the Grenfell Mission's hospital at Indian Harbour, and the "rooms" of the fishermen who come down to the Labrador every summer from Newfoundland.

Skipper Nick Smith is one of these Newfoundlanders and his room is at Cut Throat, just around the corner from Indian Harbour. He thinks it's the best one on the coast and he may well be right. There's a cabin, a bunkhouse for his summer crews and a landing stage, and a "flake"—the wooden rack for drying his salted cod. Quite an undertaking. "Cut Throat" sounds bloodthirsty enough, and God knows Labrador has had its share of murder and piracy. But Skipper Nick is a peaceful man and the only throats he has ever cut are cods'—and the more the merrier. He catches them in cod traps that work like large lobster pots: a long, straight stretch of net leads the fish into a round bag of netting, and a cunning entrance stops them from getting out again. It's routine after that. Nick himself stands at the head of the gutting line, catches each fish as it's thrown to him, slits its throat, and slides it down to the header, who rips out the head and guts and passes what's left to the splitter, who peels off the backbone. Then the cod are salted and spread out on the flake to dry. Cod cured like this are as hard as parchment and last forever. The merchants of Newfoundland have made their fortunes by selling them all over the world. Newfoundland schooners take the fish down to Jamaica and bring back good rum in its place. Skipper Nick approves of that.

By the end of October, Nick Smith can say that he has had a pretty good season, but he means to keep on with his fishing for another month or more if the weather holds up. Then he'll go home to Newfoundland to spend the winter in the prosperous little port of Brigus in Conception Bay where he was born fifty years ago. He will spend the time mending his boats and gear and selling his catch. And perhaps he'll go off to the Seal Hunt in March. But he sees no reason not to enjoy himself as well. He is a cheerful little man and a pillar of the Brigus Jubilee Glee Club where, unlike many of the east-coast skippers, he makes no secret of his liking for a drop or two of "stimulant." "A bird can't fly on only one wing," he declares as he pours his second glass of finest Jamaican rum.

He has earned every drop of it, and not just for his hard work this past summer. He has been fishing down the Labrador every summer since he was fourteen, and when his father died just after that, young Nick was left to provide for his mother, his brother and his sisters. He has done very well for all of them. Job Brothers, the big merchant firm in St. John's, think very highly of him. They have outfitted him every year with his room, gear and summer victuals, and he has paid them back every penny. He is a patient, tolerant man, proud of himself and his skills; never out of Newfoundland in his life, and never wanting to be, either. He is perfectly content with his lot except perhaps for one small thing. The best place of all to set a cod trap near Cut Throat is in the cove they call Fox Borough. Skipper Nick has never sailed to Labrador early enough in the spring to claim a fishing berth there; but in 1912, perhaps?

When Nick Smith goes home at last in December the sea is slowly beginning to freeze around the stranded Iceberg. There is plenty of ice in the water already—the rubble from the bergs themselves, and the pack-ice that has come all the way down with them from Baffin Bay. Now, on calm nights, it is cold enough for a skin of ice to form on the sea itself. The ice is fragile enough to begin with, turning to mush as soon as the sun touches it. Even the dovekies can swim through it, leaving tiny icebreaker tracks behind them. But the ice thickens as the nights grow colder and soon it is a rind which does not melt away—still fragile, but firm and sharp enough to rip through the planks of a dory. The sea gradually turns into a grey, sluggish jelly, neither ice nor water. The jelly hardens. Then the ocean swells break the ice up again. The pieces jostle and rub against each other until they are rounded off into big, flat circles with raised edges, like giant white lilypads. They freeze together again to lock the sea in for the winter, its cover broken only by tides and storms. The ice grows steadily thicker as the air freezes. Soon it is more than three feet thick and firm as a rock, but it keeps drifting south.

The pack-ice flows around the grounded Iceberg so that from very high up it seems to be forging its way back north again. The Iceberg keeps melting, and the water keeps carving caverns underneath it. On New Year's Day it topples over once again, and the roll carries it free of the shallow part of the bank. It bobs and dips and slowly spins in a cloud of mud and broken ice.

The Labrador Current catches the Iceberg and turns it south again, toward Newfoundland and the Atlantic shipping lanes.

TITANIC
V

HARLAND AND WOLFF WORK HARD all through the winter to give *Titanic* her final touches. It is a matter now of painting and furnishing her sumptuous public and private accommodations in the latest taste and style, to make her as elegant inside as she is out. All her equipment has to be tested as well: the engines and the boilers, and every inch of the maze of electrical and mechanical circuits inside her.

Thomas Andrews puts on a boiler suit and crawls through every hatch and tunnel himself, inspecting everything, from the lifeboats (far too few) to the screws on the hatstands (far too many). He does this to satisfy his own passion for accuracy. There is no need to keep his men up to the mark, because everyone in the yard is determined to make *Titanic* the most perfect ship that ever left Belfast, if only to please Mr. Andrews.

On 1 April 1912, three years and a day since her keel was laid down, *Titanic* is ready at last. There's a pleasant little ceremony, accompanied by champagne, as Mr. Ismay formally accepts her on behalf of the White Star Line. His company has paid a fortune for her, a cool two million pounds, and they are confident that she is worth every penny of it. The Line and the shipyard have grown up together as industrial giants during the last thirty years, and Harland and Wolff have done them proud, as usual.

All she needs now are her sea trials, and her final certificates of inspection from the Board of Trade. It goes without saying that she passes them both with flying colours. How could she possibly do otherwise?

It is time to go to sea. *Titanic* turns away from Belfast for the last time and sails for Southampton.

Bloody Snow

The slaughter then was dreadful,
'Tis useless to describe.
From East to West for miles around
The ice was crimson dyed.
Sharp knives and bats did deadly work
And when the day was done
Twice seven thousand sculps were flagged
Beneath the setting sun.

Anonymous ode to the 1891 Seal Hunt

Greenspond is a pretty place,
And so is Pinchard's Island.
Me Ma will have a new silk dress
When Pa comes home from swilin'.

Newfoundland children's song

THE ICEBERG leaves Labrador behind by the middle of January. It is east of Belle Isle when the first herds of harp seals overtake it. They swim past in their hundreds, thousands and tens of thousands, pressing relentlessly on to whelp on the ice in the Gulf of St. Lawrence and the Grand Banks. Small white seals with a ragged ribbon of black hair across their backs, like a harp. Further offshore, like sheepdogs standing guard, are smaller herds of hood seals, big and grey, swimming south to whelp as well. The hoods and the harps together stream past Belle Isle and the Iceberg for the rest of January; suddenly, they are all gone and the sea is empty again.

But it is far from quiet because now, slowly at first but with gathering tempo, the winter storms begin to howl down from the Arctic, past Newfoundland. They sweep the dovekies off the Grand Banks, drive them downwind and splatter them in puffs of bloody feathers against the sides of the labouring steamers. The flocks hurry on eastward, exhausted and starving, until the storms wreck them along the Atlantic coasts of Europe. Dovekies from Parker Snow Bay, blown clear across England, flutter and hop in the gutters of London.

The storms push the Iceberg along too. An eddy from the Labrador Current drags it east across the great bay at the northeast coast of Newfoundland, and the Iceberg scrapes across the edges of the banks. Past Twillingate, Change Island, New World Island, and Fogo. It slips neatly through the gap between Cromwell Ledge and Blackey's Ground. But just as it is about to drift free into the deep, it is dragged across the shoals off the Funk Islands and runs aground, for the third and last time.

The Funks consist of nothing more than a few reefs and a low, flat scrap of an island. The Iceberg towers over them. The waves break in freezing spray against it, fall back on the rocks and coat them with icicles. There is nothing on the Funks now, nor will there be for another month until the seabirds come back in the spring: only a few hundred murres, a handful of gulls and puffins, and the ghosts of the extinct Great Auks. Nothing else is left of what was once the most famous seabird city in the North Atlantic.

The sad truth is that the birds on the Funks have long ago been pillaged out of existence: first by the Beothics—the Red Indians of Newfoundland—as extinct as the Great Auks by now; by three centuries of fishermen, hungry for fresh meat; and by New Englanders who only wanted the feathers. All of them went out to the Funks to slaughter a big, fat, black-and-white bird, a murre the size of a goose

97

and just as juicy; a clown of a bird with flippers for wings, so foolish that it came waddling up to look, instead of running away. Philosophical gentlemen had a Latin name for it: *Alca impennis*, the flightless auk. The Scots and the Icelanders called it a garefowl. But to all the fishermen on the Grand Banks—Breton, French and English—it was always pen-gwyn, or pingouine, or penguin, meaning "white head," for the big, round patch on its face. And so it remained, for the little time it was to survive there or anywhere else.

The Greak Auk's fate was sealed in 1534, when the first Europeans landed on the Funks. Jacques Cartier was three weeks out of Saint-Malo with two ships and sixty-one men, commissioned by the king of France to seek out the islands of gold and spices, and the Passage to Asia. The Funks were the first of his discoveries—rich islands in their way, though not quite what the king had in mind. Cartier himself rowed ashore to take formal possession, and he and his men were astounded to see a veritable army of small, piebald men come waddling and grunting down to greet them as they clambered ashore. It was well beyond the memory of the oldest Breton grandfather that any such birds had been seen in France. Some of the seamen insisted they were witches, and that this uncanny rock was the Island of the Souls of the Dead. (Only a Breton knows what a terrible place that is.) But Cartier was a hard-headed and far-travelled navigator who cared nothing for such superstitions. As far as he was concerned, these great, tame lumps of meat were God's gift to scurvy-ridden seamen, and he herded a couple of boatloads of them onto his ships. Then he sailed westward to discover the River of Canada and New France.

The news of Cartier's discoveries quickly spread to the European fishermen who worked the Grand Banks every summer. None of them were interested in the River of Canada, but an island full of fat "penguins" was worth more to them than all the gold in Peru. It was not long before every skipper who passed the Funks stopped as a matter of course to collect a boatload or two of Great Auks, and the only wonder is that it took 250 years of these innumerable small slaughters to finish the birds off. The last Great Auks on the Funks died unrecorded around 1800, just before (or perhaps after) they were plunged into a cauldron of boiling water to loosen their feathers for plucking. The naked corpses fed the fire that kept the cauldron bubbling. All that is left today of the strangest bird in the North Atlantic is a greasy mound of soil, full of bones.

The Iceberg breaks loose from the Funks at the end of February, just as the harp seals begin to move north again. The herds have been down on the Grand Banks gorging themselves on capelin, the little silver smelts which are the food of almost everything in the seas around Newfoundland. The seals are as fat as butter by now, and they need to be because none of them will eat again until their whelping and mating is all over and they are on their way back to Greenland.

The seals swim north to the edge of the pack-ice, and then they haul out onto it. In a normal spring the harps ought to be somewhere off the Strait of Belle Isle by now, but they are south of the Funks in 1912. The storms have been very fierce this winter, and they are far from over yet. The gales and the Labrador Current together keep pushing the ice and the seals even farther south.

The Iceberg catches up with them at the beginning of March. Most of the pups have been born by then. Their coats are the purest of pure white and only their enormous black eyes are dark. The ice is noisy with their bleating wails, uncannily child-like, and with the gruff barks of their mothers. The mother seals pump them so full of rich buttermilk that the pups weigh a hundred pounds in less than two weeks. The mothers themselves go into heat and grow thinner. The bulls snarl and fight over them, rolling and porpoising through the leads in the ice. The old seals mate. It will soon be time to leave the pups and go back to Greenland. Then the pups will lie on the ice until they are hungry enough to flounder into the water, to learn to swim and hunt for themselves. But thousands of them will never live long enough to learn these simple skills. It is the beginning of March, and it will soon be time to start the Newfoundland Seal Hunt.

March is a long way from spring in Newfoundland, but the island is already beginning to come alive. St. John's harbour is suddenly a very busy place. The old wooden walls that have been swinging at anchor all winter are warped into the piers to be fitted out for the Hunt: *Diana, Neptune, Bloodhound, Ranger, Kite, Labrador, Algerine, Newfoundland, Southern Cross, Erik, Viking, Eagle.* Rugged, rotting ships, soaked in seal oil; many of them have been going to the Hunt for the last forty springs. They lie beside the brand-new steel ice-breakers that have made them as obsolete as sailing ships for work in the ice. The icebreaker is Newfoundland's great contribution to marine architecture: a steel steamer with a powerful engine and a bow sharply undercut at the waterline, able to drive up onto the ice, crush it by its own sheer weight, and slice through it like a knife through cheese. The merchant firms of St. John's invented them especially for the Seal Hunt. There are ten icebreakers now, from the giant *Stephano* to the little *Fogota. Sagona* and *Erna* are on their way across the Atlantic, heading straight for the Hunt from their shipyards.

The steel steamers are the pride of the fleet, and the merchants take care that their captaincies go to the "jowlers," the master sealers who have proved their skill and luck at the Hunt in the past. *Stephano*, the queen of the fleet, goes to Abram Keane, the king of them all—a man of many talents: fisherman, shipwright, trader, once a minister in the Newfoundland government, but always and above all a killer of seals. Keane has been at the Hunt for over thirty years, and he reckons that in that time he and his crews have brought back a cool half-million sculps. That is more than most captains bring

home in a lifetime, but he sometimes wonders privately if a man could kill a *million* seals? His one fault, in the eyes of Newfoundlanders, is that in his iron determination to reach his goal, he takes less account than he should of the safety of his men out on the ice. Not that they give a damn, as long as Cap'n Abram puts them in among the fat.

By the same token Bob Bartlett only gets *Neptune*, the old wooden wall, even though he is the most famous Newfoundlander alive. Everyone in Newfoundland knows him as a Bartlett from Brigus, one of the family whose names crop up repeatedly in the history of Newfoundland and the Arctic. No serious Polar expedition in the last thirty or forty years has set off without a Captain Bartlett in it. The whole world knows that Cap'n Bob took Robert Peary up to the Arctic in 1905 and again in 1908, and that he was all set to go to the North Pole himself, but Peary made him turn back when they were almost there. He has been honoured by learned societies for his contribution to Polar exploration and he has shaken hands with presidents and kings. Bartlett is a modest man who doesn't much care for such foolishness, but he does think he has earned a steel ship for the Hunt, at the very least. *Beothic*, perhaps, because he knows her particularly well; after all, he took her around most of the Arctic with a safari of wealthy Americans in 1910. However, Job Brothers have not forgotten that he brought her home floating mainly on her watertight tanks, her bottom ripped open from the reckless panache with which Bob tackles pack-ice. Nor have they forgotten how he tried a short-cut to the Hunt in *Leopard* a few springs ago, and wrecked the old ship between the ice and the rocks. No, we are all proud of Captain Bartlett. He is a very fine seaman, but—how to put it?—just a little *unlucky*? Nor is he the master jowler that his father used to be; his ships come home "clean," or as near as makes no difference, with monotonous regularity.

So for the serious business of the Hunt the man Job Brothers want for *Beothic* is Captain William Winsor, an up-and-coming young fellow who looks like he might rival the great Captain Keane himself one day. They hope to see their ship steaming through the Narrows at the beginning of April with a log-load of seals, sculps crammed into every cranny of her, and they are confident that Captain Winsor is the man to do it for them.

Bob Bartlett takes this as philosophically as he can. It is some consolation that *Neptune* is the finest wooden wall in the fleet, a ship that has seen as much arctic service in her time as any Bartlett, even himself. But it is his pride that hurts more than anything else. This big, tough, horse-faced seaman is oddly shy and sensitive underneath, with an eccentric taste for books and classical music which goes very strangely with his remarkable talent for blasphemy. Perhaps it is his sensitivity that always holds him back at the Hunt. As a true-born Newfoundlander, he tries hard enough to kill seals, God knows, but the part he enjoys most is the business of getting there. Any fool can take a ship out of St. John's, point her east and ram her straight into the ice. But it takes a real seaman to sail around the stormy seas south of Newfoundland to the Gulf of St. Lawrence, as Bob does every year. The rest of the Hunt is always rather a let-down after that, bloody pitiful and bloody dangerous too. A job that has to be done, that's all.

Not everyone thinks of the Hunt quite like that. Very few people outside Newfoundland have even heard of the Seal Hunt, and Bob finds it extraordinary that those who have, speak of it almost with awe; the Biggest Big-Game Hunt in the world, some say. Harry Whitney, who was on Bob's safari in *Beothic*, is someone who talks like that; he is so anxious to see it for himself that he is coming along as supercargo with Bob on *Neptune*. Bloody nonsense. The Hunt is

about as sporting as stampeding buffalo over a cliff. What is so *sporting* about hitting a baby seal over the head just to make soap for fine ladies out of its fat? What kind of a trophy is that? Nobody even uses the fur, for God's sake, though a girl would look pretty dressed up in a sealskin.

No, in Bob Bartlett's book that sort of talk is the worst kind of foolishness. It's strange that the Hunt happens at all, today in 1912, in a white man's country not a thousand miles from New York, but then Newfoundland is the strangest land Bob has ever seen or heard about in all his travels. A country born more or less by accident, grown up in poverty and neglect, and living in rags and riches ever since. Mostly rags. A New-Found-Land that's an arctic wilderness of fog, bog and rock, with only a sea full of cod and seals for blessings. A country whose first settlers were mostly men on the run from something worse: Irishmen from the famines, Englishmen deserting from the navy or the brutal life of the fishery. To make matters even harder, the fishermen were not supposed to settle in at all; they were meant to fish in Newfoundland in summer and return to England in the fall. The English fishing captains were given orders to burn out anybody bold enough to colonize the island, and they did it with enthusiasm. But the people kept coming. They set themselves up with stubborn courage in lonely coves and outports where, God willing, nobody would ever find them, and in the end they won. Once they were left in peace, the Newfoundlanders built a prosperous fishery out of cod and seals. They say today that there's more money on Water Street, St. John's, than there is on Wall Street, New York.

But not in the outports. Some of them have done well enough; Brigus, for one, where the Bartletts and Nick Smith come from. Others have not. Even today, an outporter can fish all summer and cut logs all winter, and still go from one year's end to the next without seeing more than a penny or two of real money. The merchant buys his fish, and pays him in kind. A fisherman's catch earns him enough credit for flour and molasses to keep his family through the winter, and it sets him up for the next summer's fishing as well. It is a cycle as simple and unbreakable as that which brings the seals down to Newfoundland in February, and takes them north again in April.

But not quite unbreakable. An outport man has one chance to have real coins jingling in his pockets. He can go to the Seal Hunt in the spring and hope for a big killing. A couple of years ago Cap'n Keane came home with a log-load of more than 49,000 sculps in his holds, and every one of his "swilers" made an incredible $148.36 each—a fortune beyond the wildest dreams of any outporter. Swilers go to the Hunt year after year in hopes of a bonanza like that, though they know very well they will be lucky to get $15.00. But it is hope that makes outport men keep coming to St. John's from every corner of the island, begging and even bribing for a berth on a sealing ship.

These hungry and hopeful men go to the Hunt with no illusions at all, of sport or any other kind, because God knows that if the smallest thing goes wrong it won't just be the seals that will die on the ice. There is death by fire, because wooden walls go up like torches to a naked flame; death by steam, if the rickety boilers burst; death by storm if the gales smash the ship ashore; and death by water if she capsizes instead; death, or maiming at the very least, by frostbite, blood-poisoning or agonizing snowblindness. But death on the ice is the worst of all—lost in the blizzards, like the crew of *Greenland* in 1898.

Every Newfoundlander knows about "the Year of the *Greenland*," and even fourteen years afterwards there are few families who are not touched by her disaster. Everyone knows a maimed *Greenland* man, hobbling through the outport. It happened, of all the ironies, to Cap'n George Barbour, the skipper who always took the greatest possible care of his swilers out on the ice. But he let them down in 1898, and Barbour will remember it to his dying day.

Greenland was a tough, old wooden wall, crushed and sunk now but a lucky ship in her day. The spring of 1898 was just an ordinary one for her, and the weather that March morning was as bright and calm as any of her 150 swilers could wish for. They were in among the fat by noon, a long way from the ship, when a blizzard came at them out of nowhere, almost before the sky could cloud over. It lay *Greenland* over on her side and jammed her so hard against the ice that it was all Barbour could do to bring her back on an even keel again. And it opened up an uncrossable lake between the ship and her men. The men wandered across the ice in the bitter cold, with nothing to warm or shelter them but the piles of bloody sculps. It was a day and a night before Barbour could send his boats to the rescue, and by then forty-five swilers were dead, and most of the rest crippled by frostbite. George Barbour and every man at the Hunt, from the oldest captain to the youngest swiler, prays that nothing like the Year of the *Greenland* will ever happen again.

The outport men keep coming—partly out of hunger and despair, partly with dreams of riches, but partly out of pride, because to face the dangers of the ice is the test of a man of Newfoundland.

By the evening of 13 March all the swilers and their ships are as ready as they can be for the start of the Hunt. It promises to be a difficult spring. The storms have been ferocious. *Sagona* has only just arrived from England, and people are beginning to worry about *Erna*, who sailed in January and has not been reported since. The gales have brought the pack-ice unusually far south and for a day or two it even blocks the Narrows at St. John's, something that happens only once or twice in a century. There are rumours of polar bears on it, and the papers say someone has actually shot one, up north near St. Anthony. The ice is so thick that the captains wonder if even the big steel icebreakers will get through it. *Beothic* makes three attempts to get into Conception Bay to pick up her swilers from the outports there, but she is forced back each time. In the end the men arrive by a special train, but even that bogs down in a snowdrift, and they have to walk the rest of the way into St. John's. Some of the swilers are frostbitten already.

But Skipper Nick Smith has his usual luck and he gets through from Brigus without any trouble. Job Brothers have given him the berth on *Beothic* he hoped for, and he sits gossiping with Billy Winsor and the Mate. He would be hard put to say why he is here at all, because he has all the money he needs nowadays, thank God, and he has come a long way from the gaunt boy with a mother and family to support. But Nick Smith is not the kind of man to give these things much thought. All he knows is that he's off to the ice again, as any true Newfoundlander should be in the spring, and what is mostly in his mind is the way things have changed since his first berth on the Hunt, back in '76. There's no more trudging for thirty miles through the snow to get to St. John's, and no bunking down in the crowded, stinking holds. He sighs with contentment, and when the bottle of "stimulant" comes round again he pours himself another glass; "one eye can't weep without the other." Nick Smith and Cap'n Billy and the Mate all drink to *Beothic*, a log-load of sculps and an easy passage out to the Front in the morning.

The steel ships in the harbour have had their steam up for hours by then. As soon as day breaks they cast off and race for the Narrows. There is a good deal of jostling, cursing and scraping of paint, as well as competitive and intimidating blasts from steam whistles and megaphones, before they all squeeze through. None of the ships actually collide, which is fortunate, because steel bows go through another ship's side almost as easily as they go through pack-ice. Once they are clear of the harbour the ships turn, one by one, and steam north toward the Front, the floating nursery on the ice where all the harp seals are.

Much later, as the March afternoon begins to fade, the lighthouse keeper at Cape St. Francis watches them go by, strung along the horizon in the ice-fog. *Bellaventure* is in the lead, then *Bonaventure*, *Florizel*, *Adventure*, *Nauscopie*, and *Beothic* the last of all. He radios the news to St. John's, and the men who have bets on the Hunt nod knowingly: there's no sign of *Stephano*. Trust Cap'n Keane to go off on his own. That man can *think* like a seal, no doubt about it. The smart money has it that old Keane will be the first and the only man to find the Main Patch, the biggest bonanza herd of all.

Billy Winsor has a different opinion. He is an active, thrusting man who plans his campaign like a general, with as little concern for either the swilers or the seals. *Beothic* is the last ship in the line not because she is the slowest, but because Winsor wants her to be. His instincts are just as good as Abram Keane's about where the Main Patch ought to be—better, in fact—but they will do him precious little good if he has to share the bonanza with every ship in the fleet. So he waits until dark, and slips away.

Billy Winsor is not called a jowler for nothing, and his luck holds. It is not easy to find a patch of seals, even one a hundred thousand strong, in a desolate white plain of ice which is never the same from day to day, let alone from year to year. It is trickier still when the pups are white, and their mothers not much darker. The lookouts squint against the glare of the ice and the cold north wind, and curse the snow flurries and the fog over the leads. But Billy Winsor finds his seals just as the light is fading on the second day. It's not the Main Patch, but there are enough to get *Beothic* blooded. He jumps down on the ice, even before the ship stops, to kill the first pup himself. It's one of the good-luck rituals that go with the Hunt. The crew go to their bunks content and well stimulated, certain that Cap'n Billy "has put them in among the fat."

The slaughter begins at first light. The ship is in the middle of a vast, wailing herd of whitecoats spread out over the ice for as far as the lookouts can see. All the swilers tumble onto the ice, and they spread out among the seals, swinging their clubs as they go. It is a bloody business, as merciless as the smash of a bear's paw. Nick Smith goes about his work mechanically, hardened by his years in the fishery, smashing skulls with the same indifference that he cuts the throats of cod. He rolls each twitching body over, slits it up the belly and peels the sculp away. In less than a minute the pup has shrunk into an obscenely small bundle, its dark eyes grotesquely large in the raw, shattered head. The waiting ivory gulls, as pure a white as the pup once was, drop down onto the flayed body.

He does this a hundred times on this first March day and so does everybody else. By the time the sun sets there are over 10,000 sculps heaped in pans all around the ship and a circle of ice two miles across is covered with bloody smears. It is long after dark by the time the men have hoisted all the pans on board and stowed them down in the holds. Then they are ready to go out on the ice again as soon as it is light.

Just one more day and *Beothic* is loaded up with 18,000 sculps. *Adventure*, the only other ship in sight, has 14,000. Every single whitecoat in the herd is dead. The only living seals left behind are the mother harps, who peer cautiously out of their bobbing holes and crawl up onto the ice to sniff at the blood. The ice is eerily silent without the crying of their pups.

Few of the other ships have done as well. All of them are still searching for the elusive Main Patch, but they are looking in the wrong place. The pack-ice, and most of the harps with it, have drifted almost as far south as the Grand Banks by now. Only one ship finds them there, and she is just a cargo vessel, *Durango*, on her way from St. John's to Halifax. Her Captain passes on the news but if it ever reaches the skippers at the Front—most of them have no radios— they shrug it off as a fantasy and stay where they are. What would a damn fool Nova Scotian know about seals anyway?

Quite a lot, if he is James Augustus Farquhar. He is the outsider among the sealing captains, not only because he is a Nova Scotian but because he is the only captain who owns his ship. She is *Seal*, a brand-new steel steamer straight out of the shipyard. Farquhar is a wealthy man who has earned every penny of his fortune by himself. He started from scratch as a boy on Sable Island, the Graveyard of the Atlantic, where his father was in the lifesaving patrol, and Farquhar did not leave it until he was twenty-one. Everything he has touched since then has turned to gold, and "Farquhar's Luck" is a byword in Maritime Canada. He has been a ship's captain all around the world; a shipbroker and merchant adventurer as well; even a salvage master (he used to go down in a diver's suit himself, but he has given it up now he is past sixty). Lucky Farquhar knows how to enjoy his good fortune and he has developed a taste in his old age for high society, casinos, horse-racing, and the occasional glass of champagne. He prefers to spend his winters in Europe nowadays, but insists on coming home every March to take his ship out to the Hunt.

The clannish Newfoundlanders wish to God he wouldn't. One of the lighthouse keepers on Bird Rocks, in the Gulf of St. Lawrence, has been killed in a fall. Farquhar is a considerate man and goes out of his way to bring the body home to the mourning family in the Magdalens. But that, as any Newfoundland swiler could tell him, is the worst thing he could possibly do, because a ship that has carried a dead body is certain sure to jinx the Hunt.

Bob Bartlett is not normally superstitious but he is beginning to wonder if they are right. Has there ever been a spring as bad as this in the Gulf? The northerly gales have jammed the ice into an even thicker mess here than on the other side of Newfoundland, and not even *Seal* and *Lloydsen*, the only steel icebreakers on this side, can make a dent in it. The seals are there, sure enough, and in plain view, but they are much too far away for any captain to risk putting his men over the side. Bob is a reckless man, God knows, but he's certainly not about to risk another Year of the *Greenland*. There is absolutely nothing that he or anyone else can do but sit and wait, and hope for a change in the wind.

As they wait the seal pups begin to lose their white coats and, now that their mothers have abandoned them, most of their fat as well.

Their weight is down to fifty pounds and a pup that's all skin and grief is no use to anyone. It's all that bloody Nova Scotian's fault. Why can't that Lucky Farquhar bring some of his damn luck out to the Gulf with him and spread it around a little?

On the other side of Newfoundland George Barbour is not thinking about seals at all, though the Year of the *Greenland* is very much on his mind. *Nauscopie* is in desperate straits. Barbour took her north of the Funks to try his luck, but the ice has broken off three of her four propeller blades, and she is helpless. For the moment she is floating free in between the ice pans, but it would only take a change of wind to close the ice up around the ship and crush her. A steel steamer nipped in ice is as vulnerable as any wooden wall.

The only thing to do is to repair her here and now, as she lies in this sheltered bay, though it's hardly a dry-dock. Barbour must think of a way to raise the stump of her propeller far enough out of the water for the engineers to work on it. It can be done, but only if all of *Nauscopie*'s stores and every one of her swilers are moved as far forward as they can go. It's a hair-raising decision because it leaves the ship so badly off balance that a breath of wind, even an incautious step by a crewman, might be enough to roll her over. The lives of more than 150 men depend on George Barbour's judgment, and the responsibility lies heavily on his shoulders. He shares it, as he always does, with God. Barbour is a man of strong and almost literal faith, and he prays that God will still the winds and the waters as He once did in Galilee. And He does. The ocean is mirror calm all through the long afternoon that it takes to sway the clumsy propeller blades down to the shaft, bolt them in place, and bring *Nauscopie* back onto an even keel again. "O hear us when we cry to Thee, for those in peril on the sea." Thank God and Amen.

The sealing ships begin to straggle back to St. John's at the end of March. *Fogota*, the smallest of the steamers, is the first to come through the Narrows, laden down with over 9,000 sculps crammed into every space. Her crew are filthy, greasy scarecrows bunking down on top of the stinking, slippery mess, but happy as only swilers can be when they have come home with a log-load. St. John's will be a raucous town tonight.

None of the other crews have much to cheer about. *Nauscopie* comes home almost clean, with another two blades gone from her propeller. *Stephano*, the queen of the fleet, has only 13,000 sculps in her holds. That's $30.66 a man—before kit and board are deducted—

which is better than a slap in the face with a wet codfish, but a great deal less than the swilers dreamed about a month ago. Abram Keane feels humiliated; he is respected rather than liked, and he knows he will have to put up with some broad jokes at his expense, more or less behind his back. There's nothing he can do except shrug them off, and hope for better times next spring.

The ships from the Gulf leave for home last of all. By the time the pack-ice breaks up, the seal pups are all in the water, and away scot-free. James Augustus Farquhar gives up long before this and takes *Seal* home to Halifax to clean her up for her summer cargoes. *Neptune* comes home so late that Harry Whitney's friends down in the States are beginning to worry about his safety. Whitney himself is not very pleased with his latest safari, as he has seen less sport than he had hoped. Bob Bartlett is angry, and cursing a blue streak as usual. He likes killing seals no more than he did before, but surely to Jesus he, a jowler's son, should come home with a better bloody load than just 8,000 piddling sculps. He has the wrong ship and the wrong job, and he wishes he was back in the Arctic again. Life was simpler there; it's the only place where he has ever really felt happy. He wonders if he will ever go north again.

The merchants add up the profit and loss in the counting houses along Water Street; their books tell a dismal story. *Fogota*'s was the only log-load, far too small to make much difference. The entire fleet has taken only 175,000 sculps this spring, barely half of what it brought in last year, and not even enough to cover the expenses of the Hunt. It was the ice and the bad weather, no doubt about it; the seals were as numerous as ever. Or so they believe. Nobody looks back at his grandfather's account books, when half a million sculps came into the warehouses every spring, and wonders if the seals might be going the way of the Greak Auks.

But at least no ship has been sunk and no men have been lost on the ice this spring. Some have even been saved. *Bellaventure* comes home with the crew of a schooner, *Corona*, crushed and abandoned in the ice. It is a rare year that sees more men come back from the Hunt than ever went out to it. Whatever the books may say, the spring of 1912 has not been a bad one in Newfoundland.

But there is still one ship to come in.

Beothic is edging her way along the eastern pack on the Grand Banks, about 100 miles east of St. John's. Billy Winsor has given up hope of getting any more harps, and he is trying for a few hood seals to top off his load. Hoods are large and dangerous animals that defend their families ferociously when they are attacked. The only way to kill them is for one man to shoot the bull as he comes snapping and roaring up, while the rest of the swilers club the cow and the calf. It hardly seems worth the trouble. *Beothic* already has more than 33,000 sculps of the finest quality stowed away in her holds; not a log-load, but a very good one all the same. Nick Smith is satisfied with his last Seal Hunt, and now it's time to go home. Nobody disagrees when Captain Winsor reluctantly turns *Beothic* around toward St. John's.

The Iceberg is not far astern of *Beothic* as she turns west, but it is hidden from her by the fog at the edge of the ice-pack. Feathery crystals of ice appear like magic out of the grey and freezing air, and they drop like flowers down to the bloody snow.

TITANIC
VI

TITANIC DOCKS AT SOUTHAMPTON on 4 April 1912.

Her run down from Belfast has not been entirely uneventful. The weather has been so bad that the Line had to postpone her sea trials for a day, and after that her coal caught fire. The gassy Welsh steam coal, which is the finest kind for the furnaces of ships like *Titanic*, must always be stacked carefully or it will burn spontaneously. The big heap in No. 6 stokehold has done exactly that. But there is no danger as long as the black gang from the boiler rooms keeps the smouldering pile well raked and hosed down. The problem will solve itself soon enough, as the bunkers are emptied. *Titanic*'s officers are secretly quite glad that something as trivial as this has gone wrong so early. Every seaman knows that it's when things are going too perfectly that you have to look out for trouble. Now they can be sure of a successful maiden voyage. All of them, from Captain Smith down, are delighted with their beautiful, brand-new ship.

Titanic's crew are not so sure. Their short stay in Southampton would be hectic enough at the best of times, with all the usual tons of food and mountains of mailbags and boxcarloads of passengers' luggage to be brought on board and stowed away. But this is a maiden voyage, so they have to load all the china and cutlery and linen that are part of her normal stores as well. And on top of it all, there are the special packages whose transport across the Atlantic is one of the hallowed rituals of every maiden voyage. The Purser deals with them as best he can. (Who, in God's name, needs a priceless, jewelled copy of *The Rubaiyat of Omar Khayyam*—and what do they expect him to do with it?) And there are still a million and one minor wrinkles to be ironed out before the new ship is running like clockwork.

Thomas Andrews himself is sailing on *Titanic* to take care of all these little details in person. His eagle eyes miss nothing. The crew prays for sailing day to come quickly, and a quiet crossing to follow, so they can get some rest at last.

North Atlantic

I cannot imagine any condition which would cause a ship to founder. I cannot conceive of any vital disaster happening to this vessel. Modern shipbuilding has gone beyond all that.

Captain Edward J. Smith, Master RMS Titanic

Over the loud-voiced waves of the rough-crested sea, over the billows of the greenish tide, and over the abysses of the wonderful, terrible, relentless ocean . . . .

Brendan the Navigator, ca. AD 700

IT HAS BEEN AN APPALLING WINTER, the worst in thirty years. One black storm after another comes howling off the coast of America and off toward Europe. Hurricane winds whip the spray off the enormous waves and hurl it at the ships struggling westward. The waves pound down on *Carmania*, a liner of 20,000 tons, and they toss her into a fifty-degree roll. They are death for anything smaller. They catch the schooners which ply up and down to Newfoundland, scatter them and break them. Some vanish without a trace. Some are blown south, dismasted, and drift derelict in the calms of the Sargasso Sea. One of them, *Maggie*, takes more than two months to cross from Portugal, battered, leaking, with one man dead, and after all that torture she never comes home. She is almost in sight of Newfoundland when the pack-ice catches her and crushes her, and *Sagona* arrives only just in time to rescue her crew. *Sagona* herself, brand new and bound straight for the Seal Hunt, takes fifteen days to cross the Atlantic. *Erna*, the big ship everyone in St. John's is waiting for, sinks in mid-ocean. The North Atlantic is littered with spars, ropes, planking, derelict hulks, scraps of cargo—all of it pushed slowly toward Europe by the storms and the Gulf Stream.

By the beginning of April the worst is over, and as if to make up for the furious winter, the Atlantic falls into an unnatural calm. But the fine weather has come far too late to stop the drift of ice past Newfoundland. It is a rare berg that drifts as far south as the Grand Banks in most years, and often there are none at all. There are over a thousand of them in 1912. The Labrador Current takes them south, down the eastern edge of the Grand Banks, and a large sheet of pack-ice, 100 miles by 100, goes with them. This mass of ice drifts past the Tail of the Bank and on across the North Atlantic shipping lanes at an inexorable twenty-five miles a day.

Titanic sails from Southampton, just as the White Star Line had planned, on the afternoon of 10 April. It is a majestic occasion. She casts off her lines in a crescendo of cheers, a blizzard of paper streamers and a deep boom of sirens that echoes around the big harbour. The tugs nudge her gently out into the channel. It is a delicate manoeuvre for a ship as large as this, but her Captain manages it with his usual skill. Captain Edward J. Smith ("E.J." to everyone in the White Star Line) is in every sense a Master Mariner. He has been on the bridges of bigger and bigger White Star ships for over thirty years, and by now he can handle them as easily as if they were

tugboats. E.J. is the Commodore of the Line, a big grizzled, friendly bear of a man, very popular with his officers and crew, and a courtly diplomat to his passengers as well. He has transferred from *Olympic* especially for this maiden voyage, and *Titanic* will be his last ship before he retires.

His skills are put to the test as soon as the tugs cast off. As *Titanic* slowly gets under way down the narrow channel, the huge weight of water she is pushing in front of her has some unexpected effects. It sucks at the row of smaller liners moored along the piers on either side and they pull out to the length of their hawsers, bowing toward her as she goes by, as though adding their personal tributes to all the others. But this is no mere formality. The lines of *New York* snap under the strain, and she begins to swing right out across *Titanic*'s bows. Old E.J. is as cool as ever. He rings down for a touch more speed on his port engine and a touch less to starboard. His judgment is exactly right. The flurry of wash from the propellers is enough to turn *Titanic* aside and nudge *New York* back into her berth. The tugs take care of the rest. Then *Titanic* is on her way, though a little more slowly this time until she is well out into Southampton Water.

Many of the passengers have a grandstand view of this little incident, and some of them wonder if it's a bad omen. Some people are always superstitious on maiden voyages. Others are sure it's all nonsense: anyone can see that *Titanic* is well able to look after herself in any trouble. But most passengers are far too busy exploring the ship's luxurious accommodations to give the matter any thought at all.

Titanic sails down the Solent into the English Channel, but she has hardly got her speed up before she slows down again to enter Cherbourg. She stops there for a couple of hours, just long enough to take on the mail and another hundred passengers, most of them emigrants from Central Europe. She loses a passenger as well: a man who feels unaccountably uneasy and decides to put off his crossing for a while. Then she sails again, just as it is getting dark.

When the passengers wake up the next morning, *Titanic* is moving carefully, with a flurry of tugs, into her last port: Queenstown, the Cobh of Cork. She anchors in the harbour, and picks up more mail and more emigrants. The tall spire of Cork Cathedral looks down on them as it has on so many other Irishmen who have left for America and fortune. Then, early in the afternoon of 11 April, everyone is on board and she is off to New York at last.

Titanic steams majestically along the south coast of Ireland. It's a beautiful afternoon, and there are knots of people with telescopes on every headland to watch her go by. E.J. greets each one with a boom of the siren, courteously acknowledging the salutes of all the lesser ships in the same way. A flock of gulls follows the ship all the way from Queenstown, swooping and screaming in her wake, but they drop back one by one as the soft spring evening draws in.

The last sight of land is the endless flash of Fastnet Light far astern, dropping slowly below the horizon. By midnight *Titanic* is alone, 120 miles out, heading faster and faster into the Atlantic.

Titanic is a city of 2,200 people. E.J. is master of the 700 who really matter—the seamen, stewards and engineers—though he would never dream of saying so. The rest are only passengers, but there are multimillionaires among them, as well as peers and socialites. There are rich men who have made their fortunes and, down in the steerage, emigrants who are going to the New World to find theirs. It is a fair cross-section of the world today, in 1912.

There is Colonel John Jacob Astor, the multimillionaire to surpass all multimillionaires. His fortune is worth at least $100 million, though he believes that a man with a bare million can live as comfortably as if he were rich. He has paid $4,000 for his suite of cabins high up on *Titanic*—more than most of the emigrants will see in their lives. He is on his way home from his honeymoon, but high society has not yet forgotten his divorce and many backs turn ostentatiously on him as he strolls through the ship, his new bride on his arm.

There is also Isidor Straus, the department-store magnate, and his wife Ida, a devoted elderly couple. Their son is passing them now, going to Europe on his honeymoon, and it has given them enormous pleasure to exchange radiograms and wave at the smoke of his ship on the horizon. Their steward has found them a sunny corner of the deck and they sit there contentedly, holding hands.

Benjamin Guggenheim, another millionaire, and Charles M. Hays, the railroad baron, are on board as well. So are Sir Cosmo and Lady Duff Gordon, and the Countess of Rothes. Major Archie Butt, the aide to President Taft, Colonel Archibald Gracie, the military historian, and Major Arthur Peuchen, the well-known Toronto yachtsman. Molly Brown, a boisterous Irishwoman whose husband made millions in copper in Colorado. Frank Millet, the artist, Jacques Futrelle, the mystery writer, and W.T. Stead, the crusading journalist. Thomas Andrews, the master shipbuilder and J. Bruce Ismay, chairman of the White Star Line. Jay Yates, a professional gambler and card-sharp who makes his living out of voyages like this; Lawrence Beesley, a young English schoolmaster on vacation; and Reverend Ernest Carter and his wife, taking a well-earned holiday from their slum parish in the East End of London. And down below, just above the juddering shafts, are Hanna and Soultani Boulos from Turkish Lebanon, Matti Maenpaa from Finland, Patrick Ryan from County Cork, and 668 other steerage passengers.

All of these people, even the emigrants, belong to an opulent and confident society. All of them believe without question in a world of present progress and future security. If they aren't rich today, they will be tomorrow: it is only a matter of hard work and a little luck. They know the streets of New York are not paved with gold; some, indeed, are not paved at all. But these are the people who will do the paving and build a new city too—and they'll die as rich as any Astor, sure as God. Even the poorest of them, the families from the ghettos and the boys from the barren farms of Finland and Connaught, have come a long way already from the precarious arctic worlds where men must hunt seals and dovekies, or starve. The wealthier passengers have no idea that such places even exist. If they think about Nature at all, it is only as something which is vaguely pleasant but which does not really matter, like gardening or an invitation to shoot grouse. The worst it can do is to rain on them when they have forgotten their umbrellas. Or perhaps give them a twinge of sea-sickness.

But the voyage so far has been absolutely flawless. The Atlantic is as calm as glass, far calmer than the oldest seaman has ever seen it, and the ripples of *Titanic*'s wake spread out behind her clear to the horizon. Her speed steadily increases as her engines are worked up and, one by one, her boilers are fired. She steamed 519 miles from noon to noon yesterday and another 546 miles by noon today. It is the 14th, and she's more than halfway across the Atlantic. Bruce Ismay knows *Titanic* was never meant to be an ocean greyhound like *Lusitania* and *Mauritania*, the pride of the Cunard Line, with their twenty-six knots and more. White Star built *Titanic* for comfort, not for speed. But he still hopes her maiden voyage will be a triumph of speed as well as everything else, and E.J. has no intention of disappointing him. They both feel she will do better than twenty-three knots once she really gets going. Ismay privately bets that she will have done more than 560 miles before noon tomorrow.

The night of the 14th, the fifth evening of the voyage, is a little different from the others. There is a rumour running around the ship that there is ice up ahead. It's perfectly true, and Ismay has helped to spread it himself. E.J. has given him one of the warnings that have come through to the radio room, and he passes the scrap of paper around his private dinner table. It creates a mild sensation because it is news of the outside world, and his friends have had to survive on a diet of ship's gossip for the last five days. They talk idly about it for a few minutes, some of them with a mild shiver of excitement, because it raises vague memories of polar exploration and the Frozen North. And the South too, because the sensation of the spring has been Roald Amundsen's dramatic dash to the South Pole. Ismay is a patriotic Englishman who believes Antarctica is *British*, and that that Norwegian bounder had no damn business trespassing on it. His party raise their glasses to their own explorer, Captain Scott, and they all drink the toast, hoping Scott has reached the Pole as well. Then they turn back to London gossip and who is partnering whom, and what everyone plans to do the evening after tomorrow when they dock at New York. One of the guests wonders if he was wise to have bet on a fast run for *Titanic* tomorrow, but Ismay sets his mind at rest. A modern ship like *Titanic* has no need to slow down for ice or anything else.

It occurs to none of them, not even to E.J. and his officers, that *Titanic* could be in the slightest danger. "God Himself couldn't sink this ship."

The evening is, otherwise, rather a dull one. After all, it *is* Sunday. The Lord's Day is taken seriously in 1912, nowhere more so than on the flagship of the White Star Line. The American gentlemen may play a discreet game of bridge or poker in the saloon if they really must, but the evening's entertainment here in First Class is a decorous, tasteful recital of light music. It's delightfully well done, and Mr. Hartley and his orchestra earn their applause. Most of the people in Second Class attend Mr. Carter's impromptu Evening Service—"For Those In Peril On The Sea" is the closing hymn—and then they retire early to their cabins. There's a boisterous dance going on down in Steerage, with the Ryans, Maenpaas, Bouloses, and everybody else mixed up and thoroughly enjoying themselves, but that's a different world altogether.

The quiet day has been rather more active up on the bridge. Henry Wilde, William Murdoch and Charles Lightoller, the First, Second and Third Officers, rotate the watches between them in the time-honoured way. Lightoller, as Second, is on duty from six to ten in the evening, just as the reports of ice begin to come in. They don't particularly worry him; nothing much ever does. He is a tough young man in his thirties with the reputation of a hell-raiser and a practical joker, and his career is straight out of a boy's adventure yarn: hard-nosed mate on a windjammer, shipwreck, fire at sea, even a spell ashore in the Yukon Gold Rush. He is an utterly self-confident man who believes—*knows*—he can survive anything. "The sea isn't wet enough to drown me; I'll *never* be drowned." Like every other officer on the bridge of *Titanic*, from E.J. down, he is a seaman trained in the hard tradition of the Western Ocean mail-steamers: drive on, full speed ahead, and the hell with anything that gets in the way. Damn floes, damn fog, damn fishing boats. He shrugs off the chances of a collision just as he shrugs off everything else.

Lightoller has been keeping track of all the usual transatlantic traffic passing *Titanic* or reporting in to her radio room. There are two small liners somewhere to the south; *Carpathia* is on her usual run from New York to the Mediterranean, and *Parisian* is standing by *Paula*, a German oil tanker whose engine has broken down. Another ten liners are heading west, and five more going east, through the small block of the Atlantic between Nova Scotia and the Tail of the Bank, where the shipping lanes converge. There are smaller ships as well. James Augustus Farquhar's *Seal*, abandoning the Hunt, radios her position to Sable Island as she goes by; it always gives Farquhar pleasure to report himself to his old home.

Many of the ships warn of ice ahead: *Touraine, Caronia, Noordam, Baltic, Amerika, Messaba, Antillean, Athenai*. Some of them reach *Titanic* directly. Some reach her through Sable Island, or the powerful transmitter at Cape Race, Newfoundland. The signals come buzzing into the radio room in the jerky, hypnotic rhythms of Morse code. All of them warn her of heavy going ahead. *Californian*, a small cargo liner, is actually in the ice and only a few miles ahead of *Titanic*. Her operator starts to send out a warning, but *Titanic*'s radio men tell him to get off the air in no uncertain terms. They have enough problems as it is, with a thousand and one messages which the passengers want to send to New York. But plenty of other warnings have reached *Titanic* already, and the last one is the most direct. *Rappahannock*, a cargo steamer bound for Liverpool from Halifax, finally breaks out of the pack-ice in the early evening and morses a warning on her signal lamp as she goes by. Lightoller writes it down in the log to warn Murdoch when he takes over the watch.

By 6 o'clock the signs are obvious. The air has suddenly become icy cold; the temperature of the sea drops 6°C in less than thirty miles. Lightoller is an experienced Western Ocean seaman, and he knows that *Titanic* has crossed the edge of the Labrador Current.

The mass of ice is only a few miles ahead. The Iceberg is in it, close to the ragged line of *Rappahannock*'s track. Cold or no, it is melting very fast by now. It has the winged look of bergs that have reached the Grand Banks, and rolled often along the way: a tall, central spike of ice flanked by two smaller ones, like the back and arms of a chair. It is only about ninety feet high, and not much deeper than that underwater. The side which was on the bottom when it left Jakobshavn Ice Fiord is now on top, and the black smear of coal frozen into it makes it a black berg.

There are so many others in the pack that they look like the sails of a fishing fleet. There are ships as well. *Californian* has made such slow progress that Captain Lord decides to stop for the night; his radio room closes down too. There is the wreck of the schooner *Corona* left sinking and derelict after *Bellaventure* picked up her crew near the Front. A long line of spars and planking are all that remains of some vessel known only to God, smashed in the March gales. And there is a Norwegian sealing ship, *Samson*.

She has come down to the Grand Banks after the Norwegian seal hunt, north of Iceland. It's been the devil's own season up there, and the prospects off Newfoundland look no better. All the Norwegians can find are a few pups floundering in the water, just learning to swim, so thin they sink as soon as they are shot. The Norwegians are losing two out of every three seals they kill. But what worries them far more is that they may end up in jail. Theirs is just the kind of wasteful sealing that was banned last year in the Pacific, by international treaty, and some of them think it is illegal in the Atlantic as well. The Norwegians are in fact guilty of nothing more serious than killing seals on a Sunday—something which might cost them a small fine. But they have no way of knowing this, so they keep a wary eye on anything that might be a warship coming to arrest them. They watch suspiciously as *Titanic* comes rushing over the horizon in a blaze of light.

Titanic is steaming faster than she ever has, or ever will. Twenty-four of her twenty-nine boilers have been fired up by now, and the thrumming of her spinning shafts rattles cabins as far up as the main

deck. It is twenty minutes to midnight, and she is forging ahead into the ice field at a good twenty-two and a half knots.

But this is a knot too fast.

The Iceberg is square across her track, its black face toward her. The moon is not yet up, and on a perfect night like this there are no white breakers to alert her lookouts. It is black all around. To make matters worse, Thomas Andrews has overlooked one small detail: there are no binoculars in the crow's nest. By the time the lookouts spot the Iceberg it is rushing at them from only a mile away. They phone urgently down to the bridge, but it is just too late.

An extra minute would have made all the difference. An extra minute would have given William Murdoch time to swing *Titanic* hard to port, as hard as she could go, put her engines astern and close the doors in her watertight bulkheads. He does all these things, but *Titanic* cannot turn in less than a quarter of a mile and at her present speed it takes three-quarters of a mile to stop her dead. There is no time for her to do either. Murdoch, the Quartermaster at the wheel and the lookouts high above, stand transfixed for thirty-seven long seconds as they watch the Iceberg loom up at them.

It strikes. It brushes along the length of *Titanic*'s starboard side and it litters her main deck with a rubble of dirty ice. E.J. runs onto the bridge just in time to see it pass into the dark. There is nothing he can do but wait for the telephone to ring and report the damage, and pray it is not too serious.

It might have been better if *Titanic* had not tried to turn at all. It might have been better if she had rammed the Iceberg head-on instead. The damage and the injuries would have been terrible, God knows, but at least she would have stayed afloat. But she glanced past it with enormous force, and this was quite enough for the foot of the Iceberg to rip open her starboard side in a gash 300 feet long, as easily as a knife guts a fish.

The Iceberg rocks a little from the force of the impact, spins a little, and keeps on drifting southward, changed only by a smear of red and black paint along one of its sides.

Titanic strikes so gently that most of the passengers feel nothing. The gentlemen who are still sitting up in the first-class saloon watch the Iceberg go by almost at arm's length, and joke about fresh cubes for their whisky. Patrick Ryan and Matti Maenpaa are cooling their heads after the party. They skid whooping around the main deck, playing football with the lumps of ice while the men in the saloon cheer them on. Young Mrs. Astor, on the edge of sleep, feels a faint tremor: her maid has dropped a tray, perhaps? Three decks lower down Lawrence Beesley feels nothing at all; it's the silence that wakes him as the vibrations from the engines die away. The stewards, lower still, know something is wrong and wonder if a propeller has sheared a blade? That ought to be good for a trip home to Belfast for repairs. But the engineers down at the bottom of the ship know at once that the damage is fatal as the sea comes flooding in on top of them.

The water pours into the belly of *Titanic*, quite out of control. First it drives the clerks out of their mail-room in the bows, dragging their bags with them. Then it quickly rises through the bunkers until it dowses the smouldering fire in No. 6 stockhold. After less than ten minutes the water is fourteen feet deep in *Titanic's* bows, and her stern is beginning to rise, slowly but perceptibly.

Her watertight compartments ought to have checked the flood. The manuals say that the captain can, by simply moving an electric switch, instantly close the doors throughout and make the vessel practically unsinkable, but it is not as simple as that. The gash made by the Iceberg is far too long. It is a pity that the bulkheads do not run all the way up to the main deck to make the compartments truly watertight. As it is, as soon as one of them fills up, the water spills over into the next one, and the next.

Titanic's stern rises faster and faster as her bows fill up. It takes only the briefest inspection for Thomas Andrews to know, with cold mathematical certainty, that the ship he took so much pride in building will sink in three hours at the most. There is nothing left to do but to get as many people as possible into the lifeboats and radio for help. He looks E.J. in the eye, and they both shrug in despair. They know there is not enough room in the boats for everyone on board, and neither expects to be among the survivors.

The Captain gives his orders calmly, and the stewards run through the ship, hammering on cabin doors to wake the passengers. They climb, slowly and sleepily, up to the boat decks, some with their lifejackets on, some trailing them behind, some without jackets at all. The cold night cuts through their nightgowns and pyjamas, and the earsplitting roar of steam from the boilers bewilders them. Charles Lightoller, dragged out of his first good sleep since the ship left Southampton, tries to persuade them to climb into the waiting lifeboats, but nobody wants to go. It's a long way down to the black sea, and it looks much safer to stay in the warmth of the ship and the lights. No one is panicking yet. The passengers mill around the decks, and the people who did get into the boats begin to climb out again.

The stern keeps rising, the crowd on deck stops milling around and begins to move purposefully back to the boats. There is no panic. Woman and children first, and the gentlemen behave with all the chivalry expected of them in 1912. John Jacob Astor escorts his young bride to a lifeboat, speaks to her as tenderly as he can under the roar of steam, helps her up, and stands back. Jay Yates scribbles a note to his family, hands it to a woman in a boat and turns away as well. Thomas Andrews makes sure that every stewardess he can find is wearing her lifejacket, and he does his best to get them onto the lifeboats. Benjamin Guggenheim has nobody to escort. He has lived like a gentleman and means to die like one, so he has his steward dress him up in his full evening regalia. His steward also dresses impeccably for the occasion.

Ida Straus has a place on a boat and her husband begs her to take it, but she will hear nothing of it. She and her Isador have been together for nearly fifty years, and she is not going to leave him now. They hold on to each other tightly, and begin the prayers before death. "Yet if my life be fully determined by Thee, I will in *love* . . . . " People push past them, but they do not notice.

The davits swing out and the boats drop slowly out of the light, seventy feet down to the sea. They seem very empty. Charles Lightoller, in charge on the port side, has very few seamen to send down with them, and he calls for volunteers. Major Peuchen, the yachtsman, swarms down the falls into No. 6 boat. On the other side of the ship Lawrence Beesley has stood back like a gentleman, but No. 13 boat is going down half-empty so he scrambles aboard. Bruce Ismay, chairman of the White Star Line, also finds a place on a boat, and he lives to regret it. The boats scrape slowly down the cliff of rivets. There is a hair-raising moment when No. 15 boat almost crashes down on No. 13, but all the boats somehow unhitch themselves, and their impromptu crews row slowly away from *Titanic*.

It is not as easy for the steerage class. By the time Hanna and Soultani Boulos, Matti Maenpaa and Patrick Ryan have battered their way up through the locked stairwells to the boat decks, all the lifeboats have pulled away.

The radio operators stay at their post and urgently tap out calls for help. They begin with CQD, the general Morse distress signal; then MGY, *Titanic*'s call sign; and "Have struck an iceberg. We are badly damaged. Position 41° 44′N, 50° 24′W." They send it out, and keep on sending. After a while they change to SOS ("It's the new call, and it may be our last chance to send it.") They raise the Marconi station at Cape Race, and the replies come in thick and fast from ships scattered all over the western Atlantic. None are very close.

Carpathia is their only hope, and she is fifty-eight miles away. Captain Rostron is blisteringly sceptical at first, but as soon as he realizes that the unsinkable *Titanic* really is sinking he turns his ship around. Her stokers and engineers work like madmen and they push *Carpathia* up to seventeen knots, a good three knots faster than any of them thought possible. But it will still take another three and a half hours before she can reach the shipwreck. *Titanic* cannot live as long as that.

Californian, waiting for morning, is almost in sight of *Titanic* but her radio is off the air. Her Mates are puzzled by the brightly lit ship on the horizon that has rushed up and suddenly stopped. Could she be in some kind of trouble? But Captain Lord is something of an autocrat and no one wants to wake him up. The lights disappear soon enough, anyway.

The officers on the bridge of *Titanic* do not know about *Californian* and her radio, but they do know there is a ship only ten miles away. They can see her clearly, and so can the people in the lifeboats. But she is deaf and blind to the lights, the radio and Morse lamps. E.J. pounds his fist on the rail in frustration. *Titanic*'s situation is desperate, with the water over her bows, and she cannot stay afloat much longer. Lord Jesus, is that bloody ship *asleep*? Try her with signal rockets! The first one explodes high overhead with the crack of a gunshot, and the bright shower of sparks drifts slowly down over *Titanic*. Her steam has been shut off by now, and the noise is very loud in the still night.

It's more than enough for *Samson*. The Norwegians have seen *Titanic*—only a blind man could miss her—but their ship has no radio and none of them can read the flashes of English Morse. What *is* this big, bright ship? Why has she stopped? Is she a battleship? Is she sending over a boarding party? Henrik Naess and his crew are simple men whose lives turn around the Seal Hunt, and they see nothing unlikely in the British sending a battleship to arrest them for poaching. There's no point in going any closer. *Samson* is an old wooden wall, with the usual underpowered engine, and unless she has a good start, any warship can run rings around her. They wait uneasily.

The crack of the first rocket makes up their minds. *That* is the signal to heave to and await a boarding party, no doubt about it. They put *Samson*'s engine full ahead and dowse her lights, and she lumbers off to the south. *Titanic* fires seven more rockets but *Samson* is far away by the time the last one goes up. Much later, when she reaches Iceland, her crew hear the news for the first time and realize what they have done.

Titanic is left behind in the dark.

The collapsible lifeboats are the last to leave her. Charles Lightoller and his deck gang struggle with the clumsy contraptions, trying to put their sides up; it is not nearly as easy as the manufacturers promised. After that they have to manhandle the boats onto the davits, and only then can they start to put people into them. Two of them jam immovably, and the gang's frantic heaving is useless. Lightoller lowers the last boat just after 2 a.m. The thousand people left behind watch in despair as it pulls away from them, out of the bright circle of lights. They are in God's hands now.

Titanic has been sinking for two and a half hours, and she is

nearly gone. Her stern and half her length are cocked up at 45°, towering high above the last lifeboat and rising with every minute. There is nothing left for Captain Smith to do but give the order to abandon ship. He does it quietly, without a tremor of the despair he feels, just as though it were an ordinary boat drill. "You've done your duty, boys. Now, every man for himself." The radio men send out one last SOS, then run for it. Or try to, but they have to swing from one handhold to the next to stop themselves from tumbling down the long, steep slope of *Titanic*'s deck. Lightoller and the seamen around the jammed collapsibles need no telling; the sea is almost up to them by now and they dive straight in. But the passengers claw their way upward instead, blindly clinging to the familiar ship in a last, frantic hope of living a few moments longer. Mr. Hartley's orchestra, which has gallantly played ragtime for the last hour, strikes up a hymn: "Evening." A ragged chorus of brave but frightened voices takes it up before the music dies away.

There is a crowd of swimmers around *Titanic*'s bow, all desperately trying to get away from the enormous thing looming so high above them. The people on the lifeboats at the edge of the circle panic as well, terrified that the sinking colossus will suck them down with it.

The rowers—women, mostly, with only a few seamen to help them—tug at the big, clumsy oars and slowly get the boats under way. They rest wearily when they are far enough off, and sit and watch. The bitter cold is beginning to bite into them, and they think it strange to see *Titanic* still warm and bright—normal in every way except that impossible angle.

The blaze of lights flickers for a moment, comes on again, then goes out forever. The stern rises faster, and as it comes up, *Titanic's* fittings begin to break loose. First the stays snap on the forward funnel, and it comes hurtling down onto the mass of swimmers around the bow. Then, in rumbling crescendo, the three engines, the twenty-nine boilers, the mail and the bullion, the rare wines, the jewelled copy of the *Rubaiyat*, and more than a thousand screaming people come tumbling and crashing down the length of the ship. *Titanic* stands still for a minute or two like an enormous pillar, black against the stars. Then, very gently, the biggest moving thing ever made by man slides down to the dark ooze two miles below. All she leaves behind is a vast smear of coal dust, black on the black sea, a bobbing mass of flotsam and desperately thrashing swimmers, an outer ring of lifeboats, and the big, slow, dirty bubbles that come boiling up from far below.

Then the crying begins. The first shock of the icy water numbs, but only for a moment. The cold is *agonizing*. It drives into the swimmers' bodies with the jagged pain of a thousand knives, and it strips and shivers the warmth out of them. They howl mindlessly, like animals. Edward Smith is no longer Captain of anything, but the habits of a lifetime stay with him all the same. He swims back and forth through the struggling crowd, encouraging seamen and passengers when there is no encouragement to give. "Good boys. Good lads." A child is crying somewhere. Surely he can find her a raft of flotsam . . . somewhere . . . a child . . . flotsam . . . *TITANIC* . . . *cold* . . . . The inhuman howls gradually fade into an enormous moaning babble as the thousand private agonies drift into death. After forty minutes there is a merciful silence, and all that is left is the multitude of shadowy bodies, bobbing slowly together in the calm water. Straus and Straus, Astor, Maenpaa, Smith, Andrews, Guggenheim . . . .

But not Charles Lightoller. He was right to boast that the sea could never kill him. He does not abandon *Titanic*. She sinks from under him, sucks him down and rams him against a grating; then she spews him up again in a great belch of stinking air, just as his lungs

135

are ready to burst. The falling funnel ought to have crushed him along with everyone else struggling around the bow, but it sweeps him aside instead. As a second miracle, the same wave launches the jammed collapsibles. The one beside him is upside down, but it's the only possible escape from the awful cold of the water. Lightoller, Colonel Gracie and a handful of others thrash toward it and somehow scramble up. Harold Bride from the radio room is trapped underneath, but they pull him out in the nick of time. The crazy contraption is too unstable for any of them to dare to sit down on it. They stand instead, balanced along the keel like a grotesque line of tightrope walkers, swaying, shivering, clinging to each other, trying to shut their ears to the cries all around them. There is nothing they can do but hold on and pray that *Carpathia*—someone—*anyone*—will come to their rescue soon. They lose hope as the night draws on, and the men start to slip down into the black water.

The boats do not come back for them or for anyone else. No. 6 lifeboat has only twenty-eight people on board (there is room for sixty-five), but the Quartermaster at the tiller insists that the frantic mob will swamp them if they go any closer. He is probably right, but this is no comfort to the women who left their husbands behind. Major Peuchen is on this boat, but he's no more help than a wet dishrag. The unsinkable Molly Brown has more spirit than everyone else put together, and she does her best to make No. 6 turn back. She rants and raves at the bloody man in the stern, begs him, bribes him, and finally damns his soul to hell. But it's no use at all. The howls and the moans go on and on, and the women in the boat sit helplessly by. When the sounds die away at last they weep, sing, pray, bicker—anything to blot the echoes out of their minds. They cling to each other in the bitter cold, and row a little to keep warm. "Holy Mary, Mother of God, pray for us sinners *now*, and at the hour of our death . . . . "

But there is no rescue. The Great Bear turns above them in that perfect night, without hope or pity. The curtains of the Aurora flicker, and the new moon climbs slowly up through the sky. The seamen in the boats begin to feel the first, faint surge below them, a sure sign of strong winds coming, and they wonder how long they will last once the sea gets up.

At last, after an eternity—but it is still only half-past three—there are flickers of light low on the horizon to the southeast. It is not the Aurora, but the star-shells of *Carpathia*, hurrying to the rescue. She

has to slow down when she reaches the ice, and it is full daylight before she reaches the first of the lifeboats. The morning sun picks out a mass of glittering bergs spread from horizon to horizon. All of them, and the bodies and the lifeboats as well, have drifted another eighteen miles south since *Titanic* sank.

Carpathia stops on the other side of the Iceberg, and the boats pull toward her. She lowers ladders, but many of the survivors are too frozen to climb and they have to be swung onto the deck in bosun's chairs. Kind hands wrap them in blankets and hustle them down into the warm.

Carpathia has rescued 705 survivors—a third of the people who were alive and well on *Titanic* only six hours ago. There are more women and children than men, but not by a very wide margin. Every millionaire is dead, and most of the emigrants as well. Their women sit blankly, quite unable to say anything polite to the kind passengers on *Carpathia*. Nobody is real who has not been with them in the lifeboat. "Go away. We have just seen our husbands drown."

The whole rescue is over by half-past-eight, just as the wind is beginning to pick up. Captain Rostron thanks God sincerely, draws his first quiet breath in six hours, and sets *Carpathia* on course, back to New York. She steams all day along the edge of an unbroken field of pack-ice and it is nightfall before she leaves it behind. The rising storm ahead slows her down and she does not reach New York until the evening of 18 April. Thousands of people wait patiently for her in the rain, hoping for news of their friends and kinfolk who were on *Titanic*.

The search for the dead begins before *Carpathia* ties up in New York. The White Star Line charters a cable ship, *Mackay-Bennett*, and she sails from Halifax early on 18 April. She carries a minister and a mortician among her crew, and a macabre cargo of coffins, shrouds, ice, embalming fluid, and scrap-iron for weighting burials at sea. The search is slow because the weather is still very bad. The storm which blew up after *Titanic* sank has scattered the bobbing corpses eastward in a line fifty miles long. The grinding floes have crushed them into anonymity, and the mortician has a difficult time trying to identify so many battered faces. He recognizes John Jacob Astor only by the papers in his wallet, and brings him home for burial, but most of the anonymous bodies are buried at sea. The ship's doctor does some autopsies, and he finds that none of them have water in the lungs. He believes they all died peacefully, shocked instantly into death by the sudden cold of the water. But he has not yet heard about the awful howling after *Titanic* went down.

Minia, another cable ship, takes over the search at the end of April and *Mackay-Bennett*, her store of ice and coffins exhausted, heads back to Halifax. She has 219 bodies on board, and she has buried a hundred more at sea. Other ships take over the search but there is little left to find. Everyone who died in *Titanic* is either buried with her, two miles down, or drifts on until the tapes of their lifejackets rot and let them sink at last. For many years afterwards the Western Ocean mail steamships steer well clear of 41°46′N 50°14′W, where *Titanic* lies, for fear of meeting the bodies or their ghosts. But it is not long before the war at sea makes bodies in lifejackets common enough in the North Atlantic.

The Iceberg vanishes before *Mackay-Bennett* comes home, as completely as if it had never existed. Most of the bergs from Greenland are caught up by the Gulf Stream long before they reach the Tail of the Bank, and drift northeast until they melt away. But in 1912 the eddies of the Stream take many of the bergs south instead, on unusual courses toward Bermuda and the Azores. The Iceberg goes no farther south than 38°N, 300 miles north of Bermuda, and then it is nothing.

There is a very sharp line between the Labrador Current and the Gulf Stream. It is the boundary between the cold, grey world of ice

and seabirds, and the warm blue one of flying fish and sargassum weed. A thin bank of mist lies along it, like a magic curtain. The sea on the other side is suddenly 5°C warmer, in a matter of yards, and the Iceberg's days are numbered. Soon it is no more than a lump of ice no bigger than a table, scarcely strong enough to scratch a whaleboat.

The ice is clear as glass, and it glows a brilliant blue in the Sargasso water.

On 30 April the first shearwaters of the spring are coming up from the South Atlantic. They fly past in endless lines, tacking and gliding across the westerly winds, hungry for squid and capelin on the Grand Banks. One of them stalls, turns and circles around a greyish patch in the blue water. There is a soft fizz and crackle as the last of the air which was trapped 3,000 years ago on the Greenland Ice Cap breaks free from the sargassum weed. But there is nothing to eat and the shearwater turns north again.

On 30 April Captain Gardner brings *Mackay-Bennett* slowly into

Halifax harbour. Every flag is at half-mast, and the naval band on the pier plays the "Dead March from Saul." The civic dignitaries reverently remove their hats as the endless line of coffins comes ashore. The black-draped hearses clop slowly up the hill to the armories, where the bodies are to be laid out for identification. There are few people to speak for the bodies of the emigrants, who find their Promised Land in a common grave, as anonymous as if they had been buried at sea.

On 30 April spring in Jakobshavn Ice Fiord is slowly bringing the arctic world back to life. It is light again, and the snow buntings sing, the ptarmigan cackle, the foxes bark, and the dovekies stream north along the coast. The glacier creeps down from the Ice Cap, sixty-five feet every day, and its tongue pushes out into the fiord. The tides work under it, up and down, and it breaks off at last in a crash of spray, with a roar that echoes off the mountains. Another iceberg is launched. It rocks itself slowly into stillness, but it does not quite stop. Slowly, very slowly, the current takes hold of it, and it drifts down the fiord to Baffin Bay.

Epilogue

AFTER SEVENTY YEARS, two World Wars, and an uneasy passage into the nuclear, space and computer ages, the wreck of *Titanic* still fascinates us. It may be because it is the supreme symbol of man's arrogance in the face of nature, or perhaps because it was the first crack in the self-confidence of a world that has never been the same since 1914. We still write books and make movies about *Titanic*, and a salvage team has even located her on the bottom of the Atlantic. There is talk of going down to her by submarine.

Olympic and *Britannic, Titanic*'s sister-ships, sailed on, though only after their watertight bulkheads had been heightened and they were fitted with many more lifeboats. *Britannic* left Belfast in 1914 and went straight to the war as a hospital ship. She was torpedoed in the Adriatic in 1915, luckily with little loss of life. *Olympic* survived the war and more collisions—with another steamer, with a U-boat, with the Nantucket lightship—and she was scrapped in 1936. *Carpathia* and *Californian* went to the war too, and both of them were torpedoed.

The Russian government bought *Beothic, Adventure, Bonaventure* and *Bellaventure* in 1915, and used them as icebreakers to keep Murmansk and Archangel open for munitions ships from Britain. *Beothic* became *Georgiy Sedov*. After the war she worked in the Russian Arctic for many years. Her most famous voyage was in 1938, when she was trapped in the ice north of Siberia. *Beothic/Sedov* drifted north across the Arctic Ocean, along much the same track that *Fram* and the Norwegians had followed forty-five years earlier, and she came within 230 miles of the Pole. She emerged from the ice two years later, near Spitsbergen, and was put back into service until 1967.

Active and *Morning* were used as munitions ships on the Archangel run. The theory was that wooden walls were tough enough to serve as their own icebreakers. It was a mistake, because their hulls were never designed to carry heavy cargoes in bad weather. Both of them sank in storms north of Scotland early in 1915. The Captain and Mate of *Morning* were the only survivors. Captain Willy Adams had retired by then, and Captain Alexander Murray died on *Active* while she was wintering in Hudson Bay in 1912. George Comer of the *A. T. Gifford* retired before his old ship burned and sank with all hands in Hudson Bay in 1917.

Algerine was the first of the Newfoundland wooden walls to go. She took a party up to Pond Inlet to prospect for gold in 1912, was nipped in the ice and sank. *Southern Cross* came back from the Gulf in 1914 with a log-load of sculps, passed Cape Race in heavy weather heading for St. John's and was never seen again. Her load must have shifted and capsized her as she made the turn. *Erik* was sunk by a U-boat. *Diana*'s crew mutinied in the spring of 1921 and burned her on the ice. *Viking*'s dynamite caught fire and blew her up in 1931. The last time the wooden walls went to the Seal Hunt was in 1942, and after that only *Eagle* was left. She was towed out of St. John's in 1948, colours flying, and scuttled in deep water. *Samson* was bought in the 1920s for one of Richard Byrd's antarctic expeditions, renamed *City of New York*, and did sterling service. She was eventually laid-up and left to rot in Yarmouth, Nova Scotia, where she was scrapped in 1952. Eleven years later Captain Henrik Naess revealed what she had been doing on the night of 14 April 1912.

The Seal Hunt still continues, but there have been so many protests that it is unlikely to go on much longer. Nowadays the pups' fur is more valuable than their fat.

The spring of 1914 was the worst in the history of the Hunt. This was the year that *Southern Cross* was lost with all hands on her way home from the Gulf. It was also the year that seventy-nine swilers from *Newfoundland* were caught by a storm out on the ice and froze to death. Cap'n Wes Keane, old Abram's son, had told his men to shelter in his father's ship if the weather turned bad, but Cap'n Abram sent them back on the ice again. By the time Wes Keane discovered the mistake it was too late to prevent the catastrophe. George Tuff, the Master Hand of *Newfoundland* and the Mate in charge of swilers, had survived the *Greenland* disaster in 1898, and he survived this one too.

Abram Keane killed his millionth seal in 1934 and became a Member of the Order of the British Empire in the King's Birthday Honours List that spring. Captain Joseph-Elzéar Bernier and *Arctic* kept going back north, but neither of them ever drifted across the North Pole. They both retired in 1926 and Bernier was made a papal knight a few years later, not long before he died. Captain James Augustus Farquhar's luck lasted for the rest of his life, and he spent a long and happy retirement in the casinos of Monte Carlo.

William Pirrie organized British shipbuilding during the war, and was rewarded with a viscountcy. He went back to Harland and Wolff afterwards and spent the rest of his life expanding the company's business in foreign markets. The master shipbuilder died at sea in 1924, on his way home from South America.

Nick Smith never went sealing again. He went back to Cut Throat and fished just as he had always done. He managed to set his traps at Fox Borough in 1913. The only time he left Newfoundland was in 1919, when a hurricane caught him on the way home from Labrador and blew him across to the Azores. When he finally retired in 1934 he had been fishing that coast for fifty-two years.

Bob Bartlett went back to the Arctic many times. In 1913 he was the Captain of *Karluk*, the flagship of Stefansson's Canadian Arctic Expedition. The ship was trapped in the ice north of Alaska and drifted across to Siberia before she was crushed and sank. Bob stayed on board for as long as he could, playing his favourite classical records and dropping them into the stove, one by one. Then he took his men across the ice to Wrangel Island, and went on to the mainland himself to find help. He fell into the doldrums after that—a mixture of drink and depression—but he managed to snap himself out of it in the mid-1920s, when one of his wealthy New York friends bought him a schooner for arctic work. He took her north for the next fifteen summers on scientific and exploring cruises in the Canadian Arctic and on both sides of Greenland. One of his first commissions was to build an obelisk at Cape York as a monument to his old chief, Robert Peary. You can see it from a long way out to sea.

Ralph Parsons rose through the ranks of the Hudson's Bay Company to become their fur trade commissioner, the last man ever appointed to the post. Petey Rowland led an interesting life as a writer, yachtsman and explorer. He was a destroyer officer in both World Wars, and retired with the rank of Commander, U.S. Navy. *Chrissie M. Thomey* came safely back to St. John's in 1911, much to everybody's relief.

Bob Fraser, the lookout who saw *Seduisante* go by like an arctic ghost, went on to become Dominion Hydrographer for Canada. He never forgot that extraordinary vision and was writing a book about it, long afterwards, when he died. But he never did find out the truth about Osbert Clare Forsyth-Grant.

Newfoundland raised a regiment in 1914, and most of the soldiers were slaughtered on the first day of the Battle of the Somme. The Depression and the war debts drove the country into bankruptcy, and it was forced to go back to British rule. Newfoundland became the tenth province of Canada in 1949; many Newfoundlanders still wonder if this was a good idea.

The Funks remain, and the seabirds have come back in enormous numbers, although the Great Auks have gone forever. The islands are now a sanctuary, and you need an official permit to go there. An offshore oil company tried to use the island as a helicopter pad a few years ago, but the proposal was firmly turned down.

The lives of many people were changed, one way or another, on the night that *Titanic* went down. Captain Rostron of *Carpathia* became Captain Sir James Rostron and Commodore of the Cunard-White Star Line before he retired. The career of Captain Lord of *Californian* was never the same either. He was censured by the various Courts of Inquiry, but he insisted for the rest of his life that *Californian* could not have been the ship that failed to come to *Titanic*'s help. He died just before Henrik Naess made his confession.

Colonel Gracie never recovered from his ordeal that night on the upturned collapsible and he died within the year, though not before he had compiled a detailed memoir of the disaster. Laurence Beesley wrote one too. He went back to his schoolmastering, but for the rest of his long life he had to live down the stigma that haunted every adult male survivor of *Titanic*. The stigma broke Bruce Ismay. Society felt that if the Captain and builder of *Titanic* had gone down with their ship, the chairman of the Line should have done the same. He resigned and hid himself in the west of Ireland. When he died, a quarter of a century later, nobody noticed.

The White Star Line was taken over by Cunard. Charles Lightoller, as the senior surviving officer of *Titanic*, was a key witness at the Inquiries. He did his best to deflect the blame from the Line, but they never promoted him to Captain. He retired in 1930 and settled down ashore. In 1940 he proved again that the sea could not drown him when he took his yacht across to France for the evacuation of Dunkirk. He died in his bed in 1952.

When Commander James Boxhall, the Fifth Officer of *Titanic*, died in 1962, his ashes were scattered on the sea, as he had asked, at 41°46'N 50°14'W.

Knud Rasmussen and Peter Freuchen stayed on at Thule for nearly fifteen years, made several classic arctic journeys and did much pioneer anthropological research. Rasmussen died in 1933. Freuchen married old Mequsaq's granddaughter, but she died young in the great influenza epidemic of 1919. Freuchen himself, undeterred by the amputation of a leg from frostbite, lived on to become a popular writer and lecturer, a government official in Greenland, a Danish Resistance worker, and eventually a television personality. He kept going back to the Arctic, and he died on a visit to Alaska in 1957.

Neither the Norwegian nor the Canadian governments were interested in the discoveries which Otto Sverdrup and the men from *Fram* made in the Canadian High Arctic at the turn of the century. In 1930, however, just before Sverdrup died, the Canadians at last decided to legitimize their title to the land, and they paid him $67,000 for his maps and papers as a quit-claim. They got a bargain. The Sverdrup Islands, as they are now known, are sitting on top of a bonanza of oil and natural gas, and there is even talk of shipping the gas out by icebreaking tanker through the Northwest Passage.

The lonely Arctic of Baffin, Bernier and Rasmussen is a very busy place today; helicopters and oilmen and scientists come north with the birds every summer. Peter Freuchen lived to see his Thule become a U.S. Strategic Air Command base, though it is not much used now we can kill each other with intercontinental ballistic missiles.

But some things do not change. The dovekies still come pouring off the slopes above Parker Snow Bay in millions. And the icebergs keep calving into Jakobshavn Ice Fiord.

Postscript

MOST OF THIS BOOK is true. "Most" means that I have had to simplify the history of the Arctic a certain amount, make some guesses and a few mistakes. I don't, for example, know how old Mequsaq spent his summer in 1911, but if he wasn't catching dovekies in Parker Snow Bay he was certainly spry enough to have been there. I can't prove that the iceberg which *Arctic* so narrowly missed in Lancaster Sound was *the* Iceberg, but it's perfectly possible. Nick Smith said that his last Seal Hunt was in 1912 and I have taken him at his word, though I believe 1911 is more likely. The two bowhead whale hunts happened exactly as I have described, but long before *Active* was launched. Strictly speaking, "Inuit" means three men or more, and the language is "Inuktutut." However, for simplicity I have used "Inuit" for all the people and their language as well.

Apart from that, every man and ship I name was doing what the book says they were doing, as far as I know.

Many of the most unlikely details come from the people themselves, because almost all of them wrote their memoirs. Nick Smith's fondness for a little "stimulant," for example, Joseph-Elzéar Bernier's plan to drift across the North Pole, Knud Rasmussen's trio of arctic witches and Wilfred Grenfell's rescue of the liveyere children—these are all true. Even the unlikeliest story of all, of Osbert Clare Forsyth-Grant and his pirate raid, comes straight out of the memoirs of Bob Fraser and Petey Rowland.

Much of the rest comes from scientific and historical journals, and from the files of the Titanic Historical Society, the Public Archives of Nova Scotia and the Centre for Newfoundland Studies. Some of it also comes from me, because at one time or another I have sailed on oceanographic ships over almost the entire route that the Iceberg took.

If you want to know more, here are some books to start off with. But be very careful: the Arctic is a dangerous drug and you may end up as hooked on it as I am.

Cassie Brown and Harold Horwood, *Death on the Ice.* (Toronto: Doubleday, 1972).

Peter Freuchen, *Book of the Eskimos.* (Greenwich, Conn.: Fawcett, 1961).

Peter Freuchen and Finn Salomonsen, *The Arctic Year.* (New York: Putnam, 1958).

Harold Horwood, *Bartlett: The Great Explorer.* (Toronto: Doubleday, 1977).

Walter Lord, *A Night To Remember,* second edition. (New York: Holt, Rinehart and Winston, 1976).

Basil Lubbock, *The Arctic Whalers.* (Glasgow: Brown, Son and Ferguson, 1937).

Geoffrey Marcus, *The Maiden Voyage.* (New York: Viking Press, 1969).

Farley Mowat, *The Polar Passion.* (Toronto: McClelland and Stewart, 1967).

Jack Winocur, ed., *The Story of the Titanic as Told by its Survivors.* (New York: Dover Publications, 1960).

List of Illustrations

Greenland Ice

Page 13
Kittiwake Gull. From *The Birds of America*, Volume 1, by John James Audubon, published by Dover Publications, New York. This and subsequent drawings were made by Audubon in the 1840s.

Page 16
An outlet glacier draining a local ice cap, northwestern Ellesmere Island. Note the many calved icebergs which, trapped by fast, heavy sea ice, have not been able to float away. Photo taken by the Royal Canadian Air Force. Courtesy of the National Air Photo Library, Ottawa.

Page 18
Iceberg off coast of Greenland, August 14, 1908. From *Reports on the Dominion of Canada Government Expedition to the Arctic Islands and Hudson Strait on board the DGS Arctic* by Captain Joseph-Elzéar Bernier, published by the Queen's Printer, Ottawa (1910). Courtesy of Indian Affairs and Northern Development, Ottawa.

Page 22
Polar bears and seals. From *Dwellers in the Arctic Regions* by Dr. G. Hartwig, published by Longmans, Green and Co., London (1887). Courtesy of the Baldwin Room, Metropolitan Toronto Library.

Page 24
In an ice-pack, Melville Bay. From *The Arctic World: Its Plants, Animals and Natural Phenomena*, published by T. Nelson & Sons, London (1876). Courtesy of the Baldwin Room, Metropolitan Toronto Library.

North Water

Baffin Island

Page 134

The Titanic sinking. Courtesy of The Bettman Archive, New York.

Page 137

The Carpathia picks up the Titanic's boats. From *A Night to Remember* by Walter Lord, published by Holt, Rinehart and Winston, New York (1976).

Page 139

The iceberg that sank the Titanic? Photographed near the scene on April 15 from the German ship *Prinz Adalbert*. Observers noted a scar of red paint along the berg's base. From *A Night to Remember* by Walter Lord. Illustrated edition. Copyright© 1955, 1976 by Walter Lord. Reproduced by permission of Holt, Rinehart and Winston, Publishers.